THE INNER CIRCLE

THE INNER CIRCLE

An Inside View of Soviet Life Under Stalin

By Andrei Konchalovsky and Alexander Lipkov
Translated, edited, and with an
introduction by Jamey Gambrell

Newmarket Press
New York

The editor and authors wish to express their thanks to Felix Kleiman of Mosfilm for his invaluable assistance in coordinating this project.
All translations from the Russian including afterword interview with Andrei Konchalovsky, by Jamey Gambrell, except for excerpts previously published in U.S., as noted.
Emblem on half-title page represents all the republics of the Soviet Union.

Contents

Introduction

I n 1935, a young movie projectionist named Alexander Ganshin began work in the Kremlin, screening films for the Politburo and for the "great leader and friend of all peoples," Joseph Stalin. Alexander Ganshin was the inspiration for Ivan Sanshin, the fictional protagonist of Russian director Andrei Konchalovsky's film *The Inner Circle*. His Kremlin service provided the vantage point Konchalovsky was looking for, the "drop of water through which one can see the entire ocean" of the Stalin era, as the filmmaker puts it. Though the real man and the fictional character have much in common— particularly their living conditions and their deification of Stalin — their personalities and their histories are by no means identical. Instead, the historical projectionist, who is still alive, well, and living in Moscow, has been transformed into a metaphorical Russian Everyman, the prototypical *homo sovieticus*.

The Inner Circle is not a biography, or documentary on the life of Alexander Ganshin. But it is grounded in a meticulous, documentary approach to the realities of the period in which he lived. For that reason, this book is not a typical "movie" book. Given the importance of historical authenticity in this film, Andrei Konchalovsky and his coauthor, the Soviet film critic and writer Alexander Lipkov, have chosen to present the events and psychological verities of the Stalin period, so that the Western viewer will understand the film portrays a world firmly rooted in fact. Their essay, like the film itself, is based on extensive reading of scholarly studies and memoirs of the period, as well as exhaustive interviews with members of Stalin's entourage, including the projectionist Ganshin himself. They have set the text against a backdrop of archival photographs, many of which have rarely, if ever, been seen in the West. This book should allow the audience to see the way in which the director has borrowed from history to create *The Inner Circle*.

"We live, not sensing the country beneath us," wrote the poet Osip Mandelstam in the 1933 poem about Stalin for which he was exiled from 1934 to 1938, and which eventually brought him a prison sentence (see page 39). Mandelstam died in a Vladivostok transit camp in 1938, the year that Lavrenty Beria took over the Soviet secret police, now known as the KGB. Mandelstam's words could well serve as an epigraph to Konchalovsky's film. The Alexander Ganshins and Ivan Sanshins of Russia lived in a state of virtual hypnosis, refusing to acknowledge the terror that gripped the country. They were in thrall to the cult of personality that had grown up around Stalin, and were unaware of or unwilling to recognize the hell in which millions of Soviet people lived. That hell went by many names: Lubianka, Butyrka, Lefortovo, Solovki, Kolyma—the Gulag.

Ivan (the Russian equivalent of John) is the plainest and most Russian of names. Ivan the Simpleton, a kind of holy fool, is a favorite character in Russian fairy tales, and Ivan Sanshin resembles this goodhearted, trusting dupe in many respects. Though Ivan never experiences the horrors of the Gulag (and in the film we see almost exclusively through his eyes), his innate warmth and generosity are deformed over the years by the insidious power of unacknowledged fear and blind belief: He is both a victim and a victimizer. He comes into conflict with his wife, Anastasia, and rejects any connection with the innocent Jewish child, Katya Gubelman, whose parents have been arrested. He likewise rejects the wisdom of the professor who lives in his communal apartment. His panicked response to the truths the clear-sighted old man articulates, however, implies that the spark of conscience in Ivan's being has not been entirely extinguished. In the end, Konchalovsky allows a measure of hope for the Russian people, as we see Ivan's genuine nature reassert itself.

It was not only the simple Ivans of the country who were hypnotized. As Ilya Ehrenburg,

Nadezhda Mandelstam, Eugenia Ginzburg, and many others have so eloquently written, high Party officials, members of Russia's creative intelligentsia, and many prominent Western intellectuals were also subject to delusions.

And herein, I believe, lies the impulse behind Andrei Konchalovsky's film, which is, in essence, a parable of the Russian people and their history. The Russian intelligentsia has long been wrestling with the political, moral, and spiritual legacy of Stalinism. Members of Konchalovsky's generation are not old enough to bear any responsibility for the crimes of the Stalinist Terror (he was born in 1937, in the midst of the purges). But they have had to confront the many painful relics of that history, including the unspoken guilt and losses suffered by their parents. Just as important, however, has been their need to understand the psychological imprint left on their own selves by a childhood spent under the shadow of the "Great Leader and Father of the people."

Stalinism profoundly affected every aspect of Soviet society (and, for that matter, many aspects of Western political culture—just think of the Cold War), and continues to do so today. All the great upheavals in the Soviet Union since Stalin's death in 1953 have, in one way or another, been attempts to dismantle the country's Stalinist heritage, or reactions to those attempts—Khrushchev's "secret speech" denouncing the "cult of personality" in 1956 and the coup that removed him from power, the liberalizations of the "Thaw" and the 1968 invasion of Czechoslovakia, Brezhnev's ventures into limited détente in the mid-1970s and the invasion of Afghanistan in 1979. The glasnost allowed under Mikhail Gorbachev's perestroika triggered the most thorough de-Stalinization campaign the country has ever seen. For the first time, Soviet history was revealed uncensored to the people who had lived through it: Hidden files and police dossiers were made public, and the country was finally able to openly grieve its losses and assess the damage done to its psychic fiber. *The Inner Circle* is, in part, an attempt to answer the question "How could this have happened?" and to come to terms with that historical and psychological heritage.

The healing process has been traumatic, progressing in fits and starts—and it is far from over. Just as Andrei Konchalovsky, Alexander Lipkov, and I were meeting in Moscow to discuss this book, and the final touches were being put on the musical score for the film, the coup of August 19 happened. One can only hope that it represented the death rattle of the Stalinist system. It was a desperate attempt to stop history in its tracks and, if not return to times past, at least prevent the further erosion of the Communist Party's power base. But history doesn't stand still. The coup failed miserably, and only served to hasten the disintegration of that base. Within a week, Gorbachev had quit the Party, its property had been seized by civilian authorities, and a major reorganization of the KGB and the military, the principal organs enforcing the Party's will, was well underway.

It is significant that the "August Revolution," as it has come to be called, attacked the relics of Stalinist symbolism, which, despite glasnost, had remained at the very heart of Soviet society. The day after the coup failed, crowds gathered around the imposing statue of Feliks Dzerzhinsky, founder of the Soviet secret police (variously known as the Cheka, OGPU, GPU, NKVD, MVD, MGB, and KGB), right in front of the KGB's Lubianka headquarters (some scenes of *The Inner Circle* were filmed inside that very building). The facade of the Lubianka was covered with graffiti—"Fascist Executioners," "Murderers," "Down with the KGB"—and a swastika was painted over a bas-relief plaque of Andropov, the former KGB chief and General Secretary of the Communist Party just before Gorbachev. The municipal authorities responded to the people's indignation, and immediately removed the monument to Dzerzhinsky, which had dominated the square in central Moscow for decades.

In the following days, more idols fell. In Moscow, monuments to Yakov Sverdlov (under whose jurisdiction Czar Nicholas II and his family were executed), to Mikhail Kalinin (a long-standing member of Stalin's Politburo), and to the quasi-mythological Young Pioneer Scout Pavlik Morozov were also dismantled. Some Soviet cities even went so far as to remove statues of Lenin. His embalmed corpse still lies in the Mausoleum on Red Square, however, in the very heart of a nation that is now engaged in a fearful struggle to redefine itself without collapsing into utter anarchy. It seems highly unlikely that Red Square will ever again see the robotic pageantry of May 1 and November 7—there is no longer any General Secretary or Politburo to stand on the tribune of the Mausoleum and wave to the well-organized crowds.

Stalin is dead, and in the wake of the failed coup, it can now be truly said that much of the system he put in place is being disassembled. However, its petrified remains have not been entirely exorcised from the body politic; the reflexes that led Ivan Sanshin to love Stalin above all others are still deeply ingrained within Russian society. Emancipation from the legacy of the Ivan Sanshins—and the millions of others, whose consciences were never so clear—will be a long, painful process. It has been going on for a good thirty years already. Though the end is not yet in sight and the outcome far from self-evident, this time the "thaw" has reached deep into the inner circle of the land.

—Jamey Gambrell
October 1991

ABOVE: *Lubianka Square, Moscow, August 22, 1991. Crowds around the statue of Feliks Dzerzhinsky, founder of the Soviet secret police. The statue was removed later that night with heavy equipment. Photo by Jamey Gambrell.*

The Projectionist

At two o'clock one morning in August 1935, the doorbell of a communal apartment in Moscow rang three times. Three rings: that meant the visitors wanted Ganshin. Such a late-night visit in 1935 could mean only one thing: The NKVD had come to arrest you. There was nowhere to run, it was pointless to hide. It was fate.

The movie projectionist Alexander Sergeevich Ganshin remembers that visit with a smile nowadays, but at the time there was nothing amusing about it. No one, including Ganshin himself, expected him to return. He knew that he wasn't guilty of anything, but his heart couldn't help sinking, especially since he had worked at one time in the NKVD (now the KGB) Club and he knew that it was better not to kid around with that organization. He also knew the joke, popular at the time, about the rabbit who was trying to escape abroad because a decree had been issued to castrate all camels. "Why are you running away—after all, you're a rabbit?" someone asks him. "They'll catch you, castrate you, and then just

---

OPPOSITE: *Alexander Sergeevich Ganshin, early 1940s, whose service as Stalin's projectionist inspired the story of Ivan Sanshin in* **The Inner Circle.**

---

try and prove that you are not a camel," he replied.

Ganshin expected that the car would turn toward Lubianka Square, where the NKVD headquarters were located. There could be no other destination. But the car suddenly changed direction and approached the Kremlin. The uniformed men brought Ganshin to General Vlasik, the head of the Kremlin Guard. Vlasik informed him that he was to show a film—not to just anyone, but to Stalin himself. As it turned out, the screening didn't take place that night. Stalin, it seems, had changed his mind and didn't want to see any movies.

But this event marked a turning point in Ganshin's fortunes. He was released after signing an oath of secrecy: He was forbidden to tell anyone anything, even that he'd been in the Kremlin at all. When he returned home, his neighbors couldn't believe what had happened. People taken away by the NKVD didn't come back. Ganshin had to lie to them, to invent some emergency at work. His new, secret life, unknown to those around him, had begun.

Alexander Sergeevich Ganshin was born in Moscow in 1909. He finished seven grades of school, which at the time was considered a secondary education. He couldn't go on. It

was a difficult time—there was a lot of unemployment. Many of his schoolmates became thieves and ended up in jail or being shot. He wanted to earn an honest living.

Through connections, he apprenticed as a movie projectionist in a club in 1926. He finished the course, and when the senior projectionist was dismissed for drunkenness, Ganshin took his place. During the summer, when the club would close for repairs, he'd go to the employment agency. Monday was a day off for regular projectionists in all of the city's movie theaters, and their places were filled by unemployed colleagues sent by the agency. Ganshin was considered an ace projectionist and so was able to moonlight in one of the best Moscow movie theaters, the First Art Theater on the Arbat, in the center of town. He eventually got a steady job there. When the era of "talkies" came, this was the first movie theater in Moscow to be equipped for sound. An American engineer installed equipment purchased in the United States, and taught Ganshin how to project sound film. In 1931 he was called up by the army. On his return two years later, he began to work in the NKVD Club. He then got a job with the film ministry, where he was still working that night in 1935.

Ganshin's living conditions—a single room which he shared with his mother in a communal apartment—were typical for the time. One of the first acts carried out by the Bolshevik government after the October Revolution of 1917 was the redistribution of living accommodations. People who didn't own houses or apartments, or who lived in

factory barracks, were assigned living space in private apartments by the government. This process was referred to as "consolidation." As a result, an individual, one-family apartment or house became a "communal apartment," home to as many as three, five, or even eight families—as many families as there were rooms. On occasion, large rooms were subdivided by flimsy plywood partitions to make more rooms and accommodate more people. It is estimated that approximately 6.5 million people still live in communal apartments in the Soviet Union today.

The inhabitants of a communal apartment shared a single toilet and a single bath (if the apartment was sufficiently modern to be outfitted with a bathtub); they prepared their meals in one kitchen, where each family had its own table, a designated burner on the stove, or an individual Primus stove. Sometimes even the lights were separate, with individual switches leading to different bulbs hooked up to separate electric meters. Each family had its own doorbell, or else there was a list next to the common bell indicating how many times to ring for which person.

OPPOSITE: *Door to a communal apartment, Moscow, 1990s. Each family has its own bell.*
ABOVE: *Kitchen of a communal apartment, Moscow, 1990s. Photos by Yury Feklistov.*

It was from such an apartment that the NKVD men came and took Alexander Ganshin away in the middle of the night. In the mid-1930s, late-night Moscow was wide awake. The doors of restaurants were open and the tables were full, but what was more unusual was that lights shone in the windows of many office buildings into the early hours of the morning. The whole government lived by Joseph Stalin's schedule. The "Master," as he came to be called after World War II, liked to start work in the evening and continue late into the night, and had the habit of personally placing calls to organizations and offices to inquire about issues that interested him. If Stalin called and the supervisor or director wasn't there, the consequences could be grave. So the directors of many institutions worked at night, and the staff included "night secretaries" who never left the telephone; specialists were kept on night shift to answer any questions the leader might possibly have. The entire country lived an abnormal, unnatural life, subordinated to the habits and whims of one man.

In the wake of his late-night summons, Ganshin was invited to work at the Kremlin—and eventually to become Stalin's regular projectionist. Today, in the 1990s, it is hard to convey what a Soviet citizen of the 1930s would have felt when given such an honor. It is most likely akin to what a subject of the Chinese emperors or the Roman emperors Nero and Caligula might have felt. The kings of England or France were simply God's deputies on earth, but Stalin himself was a living god. Throughout the entire country, in every newspaper and radio program, in every class in every school and university, at every place of work, people were continually told of Stalin's wisdom, brilliance, and omniscience. His portrait adorned the walls of every official agency and department. His likeness hung like an icon in each and every apartment, in every room. Children sang songs about him,

---

Suddenly, at about one o'clock in the morning, there was a sharp, unbearably explicit knock on the door. "They've come for Osip," I said, and went to open the door.

...Without a word or a moment's hesitation, but with consummate skill and speed, they came in past me (not pushing, however) and the apartment was suddenly full of people already checking our identity papers, running their hands over our hips with a precise, well-practiced movement, and feeling our pockets to make sure we had no concealed weapons.

...In the language of the secret police this was what was known as a "night operation." As I learned later, they all firmly believed that they were always liable to meet with opposition on such occasions, and to keep their spirits up they regaled each other with romantic tales about the dangers involved in these night raids....

...To be present as a witness at arrests had almost become a profession. In every large apartment building the same previously designated pair would regularly be roused from their beds, and in the provinces the same two witnesses would be used for a whole street or district. They led a double life, serving by day as repairmen, janitors or plumbers (is this why our faucets are always dripping?) and by night as "witnesses," prepared if need be to sit up till morning in somebody's apartment. The money to pay them came out of our rent as part of the expense of maintaining the building. At what rate they were paid for their night work I do not know.

—*Nadezhda Mandelstam:*
Hope Against Hope

and poets composed poems. From an early age, children were taught that they should love Comrade Stalin first, and then their mother and father. They were told that Stalin is the father of everyone in the country, that he knows the thoughts and cares of everyone. Children owe their happy childhoods to him, workers their industrial successes. He is to be thanked for the discoveries of Soviet scholars and scientists, for the unprecedented harvests of collective farm workers, for the record-setting victories of Soviet athletes. Monuments to Stalin were erected in every town, and some cities were fortunate enough to carry the great name of the leader: Sta-lingrad, Stalinabad, Sta-lino, Stalinsk, Staliniri.

In 1943, in the middle of the war with fascism, Stalin decided to change the country's national anthem. It had been the "Internationale," the anthem of the Communist Party, which expressed its aspirations for a new world community. Stalin wanted to change it to a more specifically national anthem that would include lines praising Lenin, who had paved the road to the Revolution, and himself, Stalin, who took up where Lenin left off. The new anthem read: "Stalin raised us on loyalty to the people, and inspired us to work hard and achieve great feats."

Lenin had established a government ruled by one party, in effect laying the ground for rule by one person. But Lenin never supposed that Stalin would be his heir. There were many, far more talented individuals in Lenin's entourage, who had contributed much more to the Revolution's victory and to the develop-

BELOW: *Stalin in the 1930s.*

ВЕЛИКИЙ СТАЛИН-СВЕТОЧ КОММУНИЗМА!

6

ment of Marxist theory. Next to an outstanding orator and organizer like Leon Trotsky, or the extremely educated, accomplished writer Nikolai Bukharin, the son of a Georgian shoemaker and ex-seminary student Joseph Dzhugashvili (Stalin) seemed rather ordinary and unimportant. Trotsky considered him utterly mediocre.

Under Stalin, the position of Communist Party general secretary was transformed from a largely administrative function to a position of great power that pulled all the strings which assured victory in elections, the passage of necessary resolutions, the removal and reorganization of Party cadres. Stalin assumed this position during Lenin's lifetime and gradually managed to make its power unlimited. Later, after Lenin's death in 1924, he turned it into a personal dictatorship.

Step by step, Stalin got rid of his true rivals in the struggle for power. He literally forced Military Commissar (Minister of Defense) Mikhail Frunze to undergo an operation, and made sure that he wouldn't survive surgery. He played Trotsky off against Zinovyev and Kamenev, and then against Bukharin, sending Trotsky into exile abroad, where he eventually had him murdered. He organized the political assassination of Sergei Kirov, the head of the Leningrad Party Committee, and then presented it as having been accomplished by supporters of Trotsky, Zinovyev, and Kamenev. He arranged the show trials of Zinovyev, Kamenev, and Bukharin, and orchestrated a massive purge of his own party.

The greater Stalin's power became, the more history was rewritten, and the louder his praises were sung. The "cult of personality" took on extraordinary dimensions. His political opponents and rivals were quite literally rubbed out of history. Their names were removed from books, their own writings were taken out of libraries, their faces were airbrushed out of photographs, and their likenesses were painted out of group portraits and replaced.

Of course, few people at the time understood the real mechanisms of Stalin's rise to power. People believed what they were told. In the 1930s slogans denouncing the "Trotskyite-Zinovyevite Gang" were drummed into their heads at meetings: The "people" demanded a "dog's death for the fascist betrayers of the Motherland, the Revolution, and Stalin." The people believed in Stalin the father and wise ruler, just as twenty-five years earlier, before the Revolution, they had believed in their little father, the czar.

There were historical reasons for this belief in a just and benevolent czar-father, or the Comrade Stalin who had taken his place. The traditions of slavery were strong in Russian history, and democratic traditions too new, too weak to supplant the old. It was only in 1861 that Czar Alexander II emancipated the serfs from over two hundred years of slavery; until then, landowners could buy and sell peasants with their wives and children. But even after the end of serfdom, as late as the eve of World War I, and even to some extent after the Revolution, the peasants lived a communal life. This freed them from the fear of crop failure, fire, and other catastrophes, but also relieved them of personal responsibility. There was no need to make independent decisions. Concepts such as the value of the individual or a citizen's civic responsibility were largely foreign to the Russian mind. People were alienated from political life and felt that they had no influence on government. It therefore followed that they were not responsible for the actions of those in power. Whether or not one liked the czar of the moment, it was felt that everything depended on him: bread, freedom, justice. Stalin did nothing to disabuse the people of this idea.

Ganshin was quite a practical man: He wanted to make a good living, and, well, if there were privileges to be had, why let the opportunity pass? Soon after beginning work in the Kremlin, Ganshin got married. He met his future wife in the Kremlin; she worked as a cook's helper. The administration gave him a wedding present: a coupon for the Kremlin "distributor." Only someone who has lived under the Soviet system can truly appreciate the meaning of this word. The "distributor" was something like a store, but open only to the chosen few, mostly high government and Party officials. (This system of "special orders" and stores has survived to this day.) The products in this store—caviar, sturgeon, cream, butter, and fresh fruits and vegetables—were of much higher quality than elsewhere. Everything had been checked by special toxicological laboratories (to make sure the enemy didn't poison the Party's best sons), and then signed and sealed with a special seal. And the prices were low: These items would be twenty to thirty times more expensive in a regular store.

It is not difficult today to imagine what Ganshin would have seen on his way to work every day, and what he would have thought about it. He would pass through the corridor of his noisy apartment, filled with the shouts and squeals of children, past other people's coatracks, trunks, armoires, and baby carriages, and leave the apartment. Out on the street he would run to the tram stop and jump on the crowded, moving tram. Hanging on to the next stop, he would finally push his way in. But he didn't mind. It didn't matter that he had to live in a communal apartment and ride to work on overcrowded trams. The papers and the government told him that this was a temporary situation, a leftover from the old life before the Revolution, that things

OPPOSITE: *Red Army "volunteers" dismantling Simonov Monastery, Moscow, ca. 1925-28.*
BELOW: *The Cathedral of Christ the Savior, Moscow, 1930s. The cathedral was torn down to make way for the construction of a mammoth Palace of the Soviets, which in the end was never built. In the place there is now a huge outdoor swimming pool.*

was coming to an end, the five-year plan that Stalin had declared the "atheist five-year plan." By its end, it was promised, the word "God" would have gone out of use.

Ganshin didn't like the whining of those who grieved over the destruction of the Cathedral of Christ the Savior, not far from the Kremlin. He wasn't moved by talk about the cathedral having been built to commemorate Russia's historical victory over Napoleon. What did that have to do with him? The War of 1812 was a long time ago! Ganshin was used to measuring history in terms of the time span of his own life, and the efforts of the authorities, who had persuaded the people that history began in 1917, had also borne fruit. Ganshin didn't know, of course, about the fate of the priests of this cathedral, who had been shot by the NKVD without trial because they resisted the confiscation of sacred objects. Neither did he know about the many thousands of priests who had been shot or interned throughout Russia under Lenin and Stalin. And if he had known, he probably wouldn't have cared too much: They shouldn't have tried to deceive the people, to trick them into believing in a nonexistent God.

The Cathedral of Christ the Savior may have been beautiful, but it was the beauty of an era whose time had come and gone. In its place a much more magnificent structure was being planned: the Palace of the Soviets. Its main hall was going to be big enough for the twenty thousand members of the Supreme Soviet. A

would soon change for the better.

Out the tram window he could see old churches with broken crosses on their onion domes, and boxes piled in their courtyards. They were obviously warehouses of some sort. Ganshin took scenes like this for granted. He had been christened as a child, and taught his prayers, but he thought of himself as an atheist. The new authorities had long since declared that there was no God. And now the second five-year plan of socialist construction

325-foot-high statue of Lenin was supposed to stand atop the palace. His arm would be pointing ahead, high into the clouds and toward the future, and his index finger would contain a huge telescope. The entire building would be over 1,400 feet high! Only in our great country, thought Ganshin, could you find architects and engineers capable of such amazing feats. (The palace was never built, perhaps, as some people think, because Stalin wanted his own image to replace that of Lenin. On the site of the cathedral there is now a huge, outdoor swimming pool.)

The tram rolled past an enormous crane that was lifting the shiny steel sections of a gigantic sculpture. Ganshin was always thrilled by these visible signs of the future life the country was constructing: cranes, scaffolding, new buildings rising high. But this sculpture (Ganshin had seen photographs of it standing in front of the Soviet pavilion at the International Exhibition in Paris in 1937) was especially dear to his heart: It was a beautiful, powerful expression of the aspirations of all working people. These figures were people of the future, that

new, thoroughly human type of person who would be born under Soviet socialism. It was only natural that this sculpture was made of steel.

Of course, Ganshin could see perfectly well that the man and the woman, the worker and the collective farm worker hardly resembled the factory and farm workers he knew. But that's what art was for: to represent everything in an exalted form. Art shouldn't present things as they are today, but as they will be in the more perfect, lofty future of communism. Ganshin hadn't read any theoretical articles on

OPPOSITE: *Vera Mukhina's stainless-steel sculpture, "The Worker and the Farmer." Originally exhibited at the Soviet Pavilion of the Paris Exhibition in 1937, it is shown here in its permanent location at what is now called the Exhibition of the Achievements of the People's Economy, Moscow, 1939.*
ABOVE: *Palace of the Soviets, Moscow, 1932.*

Socialist Realist art, but he intuitively agreed that art was meant to set an example, to portray life not as it is but as it should be. That went for all of the arts, even architecture. Ganshin loved the new buildings going up in Moscow, with their empire columns and huge, formal entrances. True, these entrances were almost always locked; they were just for show, and people actually used the narrow back entries. But Ganshin didn't mind, he didn't even think about it—it was enough that the facade of the building showed things in the grand style of the future society.

Ganshin also knew, of course, that it was not as simple to plow the fields as it was in the films he showed, such as *The Tractor Drivers*. He knew that Soviet tanks weren't as powerful as they seemed on the screen (after all, he'd served in the army himself), that they couldn't fell tall trees at a single go. But that didn't

ABOVE: *Late-afternoon rush hour on the tram. Moscow, ca. late 1920s/early 1930s.*
OPPOSITE: *Trams near the Hotel Metropol, central Moscow, ca. late 1920s/early 1930s.*

interfere with his belief in what he saw. The movies were special. They showed a better, perfected life, the life the country might live in another ten years or so.

And even when it wasn't a matter of art but of more or less documentary images, such as photographs in the newspapers and journals, Ganshin wasn't bothered by the fact that they were usually staged and that the people in them stood, sat, or worked in unnatural poses. After all, if you just photographed any which way, then the picture wouldn't come out right, it wouldn't show life the way it ought to look.

Ganshin would ride the tram to Three Stations Square and then get on the metro at Komsomolskaya station. It was named in honor of the builders of the Moscow metro, the heroic Komsomol (Communist Youth Organization) workers. They had worked like shock workers to fulfill Stalin's directive to build the best, most beautiful metro in the world. (There were some Komsomol workers who participated in the construction of the metro, of course, but there were far more political prisoners under the guard of the NKVD; no one knows how many people perished from the lack of elementary machinery and bad ventilation.) The metro was named in honor of Lazar Kaganovich, "Iron Lazar," the People's Commissar of Communications and Transportation, one of Stalin's closest associates. Thanks to Kaganovich's energetic direction, the papers said, the first stations had opened on schedule.

The metro was indeed impressive, with its marble columns holding up high vaults, its

ABOVE: *Figure of a "student" from the Revolution Square Metro Station, Moscow, 1938.*

LEFT: *Mosaic showing a collective farmworker, from Mayakovsky Metro Station, Moscow.*

OPPOSITE: *View of Revolution Square Metro Station, Moscow, opened in 1938. The figures are made of bronze, and the niches of red stone. Construction began on the Moscow metro in 1932, and the first station was opened in 1935.*

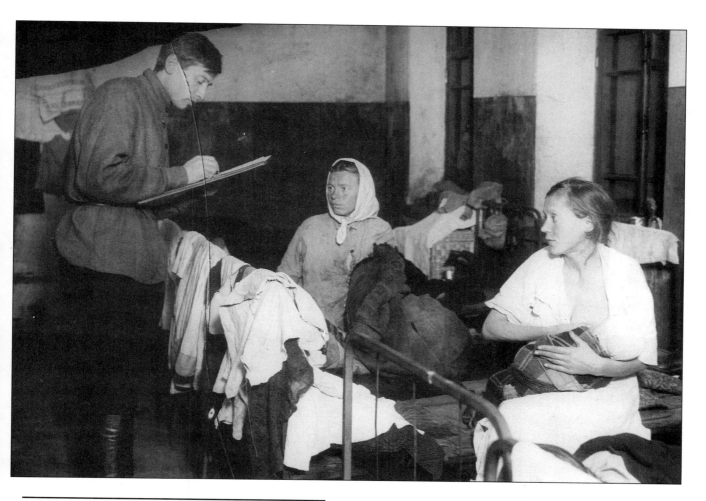

OPPOSITE: *Mother and two children in workers' dorm or apartment, Moscow, 1923. This kind of stove was called a "burzhuika" or "bourgeoise." Made from a barrel, it burned books, paper, bits of furniture and other odds and ends, heating up to red hot quite quickly on very little fuel.*

ABOVE: *Registration of the population at a flophouse, 1918.*

RIGHT: *Woman washing clothes, probably in a communal apartment, 1930s. The traditional stove, at right, was called a "Dutch" stove; apartments such as this were not equipped with a bathroom, and so all washing and cooking were done in the kitchen. Note the teapot and child's potty on the sled against the wall.*

LEFT: *Khitrov Market, Manezh Square, Moscow, early 1930s. The former upper and middle classes were forced to sell off many of their belongings in order to buy food and heating fuel, which were in short supply. These kinds of markets were also popular because of the lack of goods in stores; Khitrov Market was closed down in the mid-1930s.*

BELOW: *Workers receiving bread ration, Chapaevsk, 1931. The standard bread ration for a working person at the time was about 1 lb. a day; non-working dependents and children received less. The man behind the counter is tearing off the coupon for that day's bread ration.*

OPPOSITE, TOP: *Alexander Laktionov,* **"Moving into a New Apartment."** *Note the portrait of Stalin. After 1956, this popular painting was only reproduced as a detail, and Stalin's image was cropped out.*

OPPOSITE, BOTTOM: *Family moving into an apartment in a new building, 1929.*

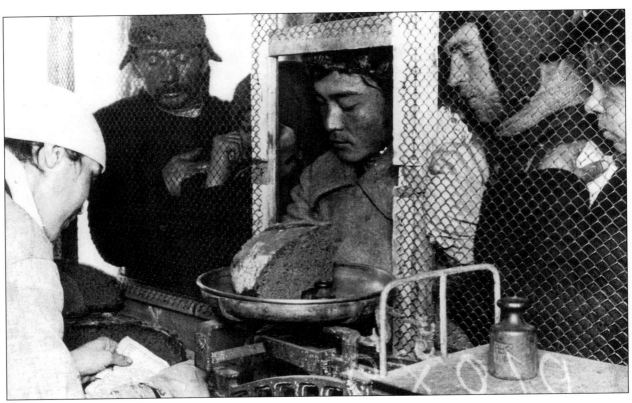

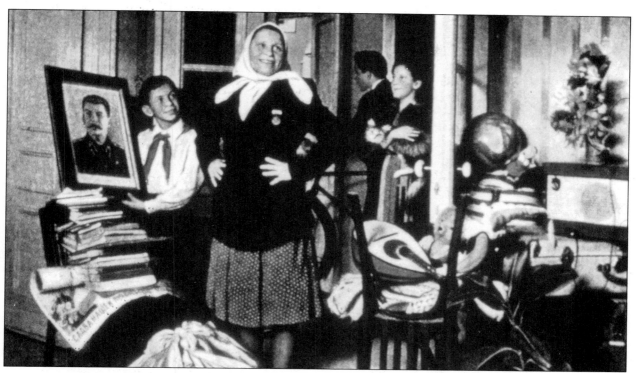

19

ПЛАМЕННЫЙ ПРИВЕТ ЛУЧШЕМУ ДРУГУ ФИЗКУЛЬТУРНИКО

magnificent porcelain *panneaux*, mosaics, bronze sculptures, and its clean, bright electric light.

Each subway station was different, each was an underground palace built by the country's best architects. The subway was the incarnation of the country's dreams for the future. Ganshin's two favorite subway stations were Mayakovsky Square and Revolution Square. Mayakovsky Square was truly worthy of the great Russian poet himself. It was full of energy, strength, movement. Ganshin liked the graceful stainless-steel arches of the ceiling, rising like the vaults of the sky itself. A wonderful material— steel! No wonder Comrade Stalin had chosen this ascetic, powerful pen name. (*Stal'* means steel in Russian.) Yes, the people who had made the revolution must have been made out of that material themselves. These were the new kind of people whom socialism was creating—strong and invincible, like the athletes on the mosaics in the Mayakovsky Square station.

Ganshin liked to look at the bronze sculptures of the sailors, soldiers, workers, and parachutists at Revolution Square. Their figures conveyed an appropriate feeling of tension, severity, readiness. It was a difficult, severe time in the country's history; enemies had surrounded them and were just waiting to destroy the first Socialist Revolution. We can only rely, Ganshin thought, on the bayonet and revolver—otherwise our enemies will destroy the people's leaders, blow up the metro, and wipe away everything that has been achieved with such difficulty since the Revolution.

From Revolution Square it was a short walk

ABOVE: *Mass sports and physical education demonstration on Red Square, 1936. The banner over the portrait of Stalin reads: "Life has become better, comrades. Life has become happier."*
OPPOSITE, TOP: *Stalin and members of the Politburo on Lenin's mausoleum tribune, May 1, 1936.*
OPPOSITE, BOTTOM: *Demonstration, Red Square, 1936.*

to the Kremlin, to the gates of Spasskaya Tower. Passing by Lenin's mausoleum on Red Square, Ganshin would usually slow down. He always experienced a feeling of exaltation when he saw the unending chain of people from all corners of the country and the world, who had come to Moscow to pay their respects to the great Lenin, lying as real as life in his transparent sarcophagus. On the May 1 and November 7 holidays, Stalin and the Politburo would appear on the tribune of the mausoleum to greet the marching columns of workers. The very spot on which the leadership stood symbolized their closeness to Lenin.

It wasn't publicly known that Lenin's widow, Nadezhda Krupskaya, had strongly protested this viola-

The most impressive feature of the Red Square celebration to me personally was the demonstration of the marching workers both during and after the military exhibition. Interspersed among the regular military units reviewed by Marshal Voroshilov, there were approximately several thousand civilians who marched in company formation armed with rifles....From 12:30 on throughout the whole afternoon, however, the entire Red Square was jammed with the civilian marching populace (workingmen's clubs) who entered the Red Square simultaneously from three converging streets. The streets were jammed for miles with the crowds which had been marching all morning and which would be marching all through the afternoon in order to pass before the reviewing stand in front of the Kremlin. Within the Square itself there was a perfect sea of standards, transparencies, banners with slogans, and small allegorical models and statues which were being carried by thousands of apparently enthusiastic marchers. It was a mixed crowd of both sexes and all ages and there were many babies and small children carried on the shoulders of parents so that they might catch a glimpse of Stalin.

—*Joseph E. Davies:* **Mission to Moscow**

tion of Lenin's last wishes. It is said that he had asked to be buried in the cemetery next to

Later we went to Red Square, where a queue of people at least a quarter of a mile long stood waiting to go through Lenin's tomb. In front of the door of the tomb two young soldiers stood like wax figures. We could not even see that they blinked their eyes. All afternoon, and nearly every afternoon, a slow thread of people marches through the tomb to look at the dead face of Lenin in his glass casket; thousands of people, and they move past the glass casket and look for a moment on the domed forehead and the sharp nose and the pointed chin of Lenin. It is like a religious thing, although they would not call it religious.

—*John Steinbeck:* **A Russian Journal**

his mother. It was Stalin, not Lenin, who needed this waxlike mummy. He needed the tribune for pomp and parades, needed the ritual processions past the mausoleum. The hourly changing of the mausoleum honor guard—all fine young fellows with strong Russian and Ukrainian faces, handpicked, well trained, none shorter than six feet—affirmed the continuity of power and the seriousness of purpose at the very heart of the country and the government. By deifying the dead Lenin, Stalin could undertake his own self-deification.

OPPOSITE: *Aerial view of the Lenin mausoleum, 1936.*
BELOW: *Painting representing an idealized version of Lenin and Stalin's first meeting.*

Cinema: The Most Important Art of All

Ganshin liked the banners quoting Lenin that hung in all the movie theaters and clubs where he worked: "Of All the Arts, the Cinema Is the Most Important!" That meant he was involved in momentous affairs. The arts were important. After all, Stalin had called writers the engineers of human souls. The government knew that the development of a new type of human being depended on the books he read, and even more, on the films he saw. After all, the movies were readily accessible to the entire population.

Thus it was not surprising that Comrade Stalin paid so much attention to the cinema. He didn't watch movies just for fun. This was serious business. Sometimes he would show films to guests after a meeting. Meetings in the Kremlin usually ended quite late, about 11 P.M. After that, Stalin and the members of the Politburo would stroll around the Kremlin grounds to get some fresh air. Then they would return to the screening room.

A large country like the USSR, with a domestic market of more than two hundred million people, should have been able to produce two hundred to three hundred films a year. But the highly centralized, government-controlled Soviet film industry held steady throughout the 1920s at about forty films a year. By the end of the Stalin era the number of films had been reduced to a dozen or so per annum. The thinking was that it was better to produce only a few films, but films of the highest ideological-artistic quality. Each movie should serve as a role model that simple Soviet people could emulate in their everyday lives. Because of this, entire film studios stood idle. Directors, cameramen, editors, scriptwriters, and technical personnel received a salary to do nothing. The country's best directors waited years for the opportunity to produce anything at all; young filmmakers had nothing to look forward to—they were forever stuck as assistants.

If movies were an affair of state, clearly they should be governed accordingly. In addition to the government-owned film studios in Moscow, Leningrad, Kiev, Tbilisi, Erevan, and elsewhere, there was the Central Film Industry Directorate. This, in effect, was a censorship ministry with its own staff of "editors" who went over every screenplay put into production and every finished film with a fine-tooth

OPPOSITE: *Stalin's screening room in the film* **The Inner Circle;** *the set is an exact reproduction of the Kremlin room where Ganshin showed movies to Stalin.* *(Photo © 1991 by Columbia Pictures.)*

comb, looking for ideological "errors." The head of the directorate held an important position, with the status of a minister, and much more direct access to Stalin than most other ministers had. (The ministry was reformed periodically and its name changed, but the censorship function remained the same. The most recent incarnation was Goskino.)

During his Kremlin service as Stalin's film projectionist, Ganshin worked under three "ministers." The first, Boris Shumiatsky, an Old Bolshevik (i.e., a member of the Party before the Revolution), was arrested and shot as an enemy of the people by the NKVD under Nikolai Ezhov. The second, Dukelsky, who came to the post from the NKVD, tried, with some success, to establish the same order in the film industry. To the delight of filmmak-

My father would leave late to spend the night at Kuntsevo. Sometimes before he left he'd come to my room in his overcoat to kiss me good night as I lay sleeping. He liked kissing me while I was little, and I'll never forget how tender he was to me. It was the warm Georgian tenderness to children.

It was in these years that my father started taking me to the movies and the theater. The ones we went to most often were the Moscow Art Theater, the Maly, the Bolshoi and the Vakhtangov. We saw *The Hot Heart, Yegor Bulychov, Lyubov Yarovaya* and *Platon Krechet.* And we heard *Boris Godunov, Sadko* and *Ivan Susanin* at the opera. My father went to the theater a good deal before the war. Usually we went in a group. They'd put me in the front row of the box. My father would sit somewhere way in back.

But the movies were what thrilled me most of all. There was a theater in the Kremlin, on the site of what had once been the Winter Garden, with passageways linking it to the old Kremlin Palace. We used to go after dinner, about nine in the evening. It was late for me, of course, but I begged so hard that my father couldn't refuse. He'd push me in front and say with a laugh, "You show us how to get there, Housekeeper. Without you to guide us we'd never find it!" I'd lead a whole long procession to the other end of the deserted Kremlin. Behind us came the many members of the bodyguard and the heavy armored cars crawling at a snail's pace. We generally saw two movies, maybe more, and stayed till two in the morning....

So many wonderful movies were shown for the first time on the little screen in the Kremlin! There were *Chapayev*, the Gorky trilogy, films about Peter the Great, *Circus* and *Volga-Volga*. All the best Soviet films were launched in that hall in the Kremlin. At first it was Boris Zakharovich Shumiatsky who used to present them to the government. Later it was Dukelsky and later, for many years, I. G. Bolshakov.

In those days, before the war, it wasn't yet the custom for the Party to criticize films and insist that they be remade. They were seen, approved and then released for public distribution. Even if something wasn't quite right, nothing happened to the movie or those who had made it. It was only after the war that it became customary to denounce nearly every new film that was made.

I'd get out of the movie late and go racing home through the empty, quiet Kremlin. The next day at school I could think of nothing but the heroes I'd seen on film the night before.

My father thought it was better for me to watch movies than to sit at home. Possibly he didn't even think whether it would be better for me or not. Maybe he just liked having me along. I amused and diverted him, and was a comfort to him besides.

—*Svetlana Alliluyeva:*
Twenty Letters to a Friend

ers, he was transferred to the Navy (his most important qualification being his Party loyalty). The third, Ivan Bolshakov, managed to keep his job, though he walked in a virtual minefield during the entire fifteen years he worked for Stalin. Bolshakov survived because he correctly understood what was most important in his job.

Stalin saw every film produced, and personally decided the fate of each one. His was the only opinion that counted in the movie business. Although as minister, it was formally Bolshakov's responsibility to make the decision to release a film, he never tried to do so himself. With simplehearted candor he would say to a director inquiring about the fate of his film: "I don't yet know what my opinion of your film is." Bolshakov's main job was to show films to Stalin. This was an art in and of itself, and Bolshakov, an experienced apparatchik, was a master of it.

When the hot line rang at the movie ministry in central Moscow, Bolshakov would rush off, saying, "I'm leaving." Everyone in Goskino knew that there would be a screening in the Kremlin that night. Two black limousines accompanied by a KGB colonel would take the sealed film canisters to the Kremlin (they were sealed to ensure that no bombs could be hidden in them). Bolshakov never went to the Kremlin with only one film: You could never know what the Master's mood would be, so it was wise to have a selection on hand. If, let's say, the Master were in a bad mood and his leg ached, Bolshakov would never show a new movie. He would lie and say that there was nothing new out yet, and would show a Soviet film that he already knew Stalin liked. If Stalin didn't want to see the Soviet picture, then foreign films were brought out. Jean Duvivier's 1938 film *The Great Waltz* and Charlie Chaplin's *Modern Times* and *City Lights*, in particular, were among his favorites.

However, Stalin strongly disliked Chaplin's *The Dictator*, and it was never shown in the USSR, even though during the war Chaplin donated copies to the Allies. But Stalin did like *Modern Times* and *City Lights*. The Master also enjoyed gangster films: James Cagney was his favorite foreign actor. Perhaps Stalin was impressed by his small stature and almost Russian-looking face.

Ganshin explains the fact that Stalin reviewed every film by the lack of intelligent people in the ministry review committees. No one wanted to take responsibility he says; everyone rushed to dump all the work on Stalin. According to Ganshin, that's what happened with the second part of Sergei Eisenstein's *Ivan the Terrible*. They were scared to release the film, in which the character Maliuta Skuratov beheads all the boyars. But, says Ganshin, Stalin watched it and said, "Excuse me, but what was he supposed to do when the country was being torn to pieces, ripped into separate princedoms? That's what made Ivan the Terrible so great, he united them! How could he do otherwise?" Stalin ordered that the film be released, according to Ganshin.

Apparently Ganshin has forgotten much of what went on in those years, and there was much he knew only secondhand. The story of *Ivan the Terrible,* Part II, is in fact quite different. The film was banned. Eisenstein died without managing to make a new version acceptable to Stalin. A special resolution was issued by the Central Committee, in which the film's ideological mistakes were enumerated: Eisenstein had depicted Czar Ivan as a weak-willed Hamlet, and his "progressive" oprichniki as a gang of Ku Klux Klansmen. There exists a record of Stalin's views on *Ivan the Terrible,* made by Eisenstein himself just after

That evening in 1934 the decisive screening [of Kozintsev's film *Maxim's Youth*] was supposed to take place...

Boris Zakharovich Shumiatsky, the director of cinema at the time, rode in the car with one of his assistants, Trauberg and me....We drove over the little bridge leading to the Kremlin gates....Suddenly, without any transition, literally within a minute, we found ourselves in another world. We had just passed through the crowded Moscow streets where trams and cars rushed about, the familiar life of the country where I was born, grew up and worked surrounded me. But here, illuminated by the cold light of tall lampposts, was an immense square, and not a soul was to be seen on it. The huge cathedral towers shone white against a black sky. Everything was perfectly clean and mute. As if in a dream, places suddenly appeared that I had once seen in photographs in the magazine *Niva*, but that I had long since forgotten. And now they were at hand. I could reach out and touch them: the Czar Cannon, the Czar Bell.

Shumiatsky opened the silent entry doors: we were in an enormous vestibule. There was no one in sight. We walked through deserted, sterile hallways and high, narrow corridors; you could sense the thickness of the walls, the carpets rendered our steps soundless. We moved in a vacuum. Occasionally, in the open door of a far-off room, a figure in army uniform would appear and disappear, further intensifying the feeling of utter emptiness. Slowly, as in a dream, a man materialized: he hung his coat silently on a coat rack, looked at us (or rather, through us) with unseeing eyes, and went on. Shumiatsky disappeared and then reappeared. With a worried face he led us somewhere up a staircase. It was easier to breath here in the projectionist's booth.

"We'll wait," said Shumiatsky in a tense whisper. "They'll call us."

A full-length documentary film was being shown. Time stretched out endlessly. At that moment I understood quite well the justice of the request to make shorter films.

A man appeared in the doorway, and Shumiatsky's face grew even more worried.

"It's time," the man said quickly and quietly. "Follow me." And once again we moved through empty, silent corridors. Shumiatsky stopped before one of the doors. He slowed down, like a swimmer about to dive into icy water, and grabbed the door handle.

Maxim's Youth was shown in a large hall. The sound wasn't very good. In those days the sound was regulated by a mixer placed in the screening room: a turn of the lever would make the sound louder or weaker. I approached the mix machine on tiptoe; the back row was occupied by army officers. The man at the machine silently yielded his place to me. While I figured out how the sound control panel worked my eyes grew accustomed to the darkness. There were several soft armchairs in the room. The armrests were big, the backs high: you couldn't see the people in the chairs. Occasionally you could hear a word or two from behind the chair backs.

"The authors are here," I heard a voice with a Georgian accent say, "so critical remarks can be made at the end."

Trauberg and I looked at each other.

We heard the voice several times during the screening. I listened hard to the words, trying to understand their meaning. It wasn't easy: sharp, at times even indignant exclamations were followed by approving interjections. But neither the anger nor the praise had any relation to the quality of the film. Gradually I realized that Stalin didn't watch movies as works of art. He watched them as though they were real events taking place before his eyes, the real actions of people—beneficial or destructive—and he immediately gave vent to his irritation if the people on the screen didn't work well, say, or praised them when they acted correctly.

—*Grigory Kozintsev:* The Deep Screen

his conversation with Stalin in the Kremlin, and its tone is far from favorable. "One of Ivan the Terrible's mistakes," Stalin said at the time, "was that he didn't kill off the five main feudal families. If he had destroyed these five families, then the Time of Trouble wouldn't have happened. But Ivan the Terrible executed a few people and then spent a long time repenting and praying. God got in his way in this affair. He should have been more decisive." The second part of *Ivan the Terrible* was released only five years after Stalin's death.

Stalin saw the movies as a political tool. They were supposed to be propaganda, to make people believe whatever would advance his own political line. The viewer was supposed to watch entertaining films about the happy life of the Soviet people and sing along with the films' heroes, "How good it is to live in the land of the Soviets!" Films about the Russian czars Peter the Great and Ivan the Terrible should convince him that the task of building a great Russia requires that everyone submit to the will of the state, that all sacrifices and victims are acceptable in the name of creating a "great Russian kingdom"! He should watch films about Comrade Stalin and realize how lucky the people were to have such a wise, brilliant leader.

In contrast to Hitler, who liked to see himself in documentary films and newsreels, Stalin preferred fictional films. In fictional films he could be presented in a far more flattering manner than in real life. Although photographs and portraits in the press and elsewhere depicted Stalin as an imposing physical presence, he was in fact only five-three. He avoided being photographed next to people taller than he, and when he reviewed parades from the tribune of Lenin's mausoleum, he stood on a special bench. Furthermore, one of his arms was shorter than the other (the result of a birth

defect), his face was covered with smallpox scars, and his teeth were crooked and yellowed. But in the movies, the cult of personality could find its ideal expression. A series of charming actors—primarily Mikhail Gelovani and Alexei Dikii—portrayed Stalin as a handsome, noble character. Stalin's role in the pre-Revolutionary underground, the October Revolution, the Civil War, and World War II were also mythologized by the movies. All the victories of those years were presented as Stalin's personal achievements. Lenin's role was downplayed, while Trotsky, Bukharin, Zinovyev, Kamenev, and other important revolutionaries were openly vilified. The people, accustomed to defer to the top authority for centuries, accepted these cinematic icons as an entirely natural substitute for the previous adulation of the czar. The movies portrayed Stalin as simple people wanted to see him: wise, perspicacious, fatherly, concerned, sincere, humble.

The playwright Iosif Prut, who happened to be in the room when director Mikhail Chiaureli screened the film *Oath* for Stalin, tells the following story. When the actor playing Stalin kissed the hand of the actress Giatsintova in the role of mother of a large working family (her part was an allegory of the Socialist Realist "Motherland"), Stalin muttered indignantly: "That's not right. I've never kissed a woman's hand in my life." To which Chiaureli replied calmly, "The people know better what Comrade Stalin does and doesn't do."

Stalin instructed filmmakers on the themes appropriate for their films, and the proper interpretation of historical events. This was usually done through intermediaries, but sometimes personally. Once, after a screening, Stalin drove Alexander Dovzhenko, director of the film *Shchors*, home. They spent a long time walking around the courtyard, to the hor-

OPPOSITE: *Mass swim, demonstration of sailors in honor of Stalin, Sevastopol, 1950; the banner under the central portrait reads, "Glory to the Great Stalin."* ABOVE: *Train engine named "Joseph Stalin."*

a.

b.

c.

Monuments to Stalin such as these could be found all over the country. In the late 1950s, they were dismantled and destroyed or put in storage.

a. *All-Union Agricultural Exhibition (now Achievements of the People's Economy Exhibition), Moscow, 1949.*

b. *Bolshaya Volga, 1952.*

c. *Azovstal Factory, Ukraine, 1937.*

d. *Frunze (now Bishkek), 1940.*

e. *Volga-Don Canal, 1930s.*

f. *Village of Dikson in the far north, 1947.*

g. *Stalinsk, 1949.*

d.

e.

f.

g.

othing in the Soviet Union goes on outside the vision of the plaster, bronze, painted or embroidered eye of Stalin. His portrait hangs not only in every museum, but in every room of every museum. His statue marches in front of all public buildings. His bust is in front of all airports, railroad stations, bus stations. His bust is also in all schoolrooms, and his portrait is often directly behind his bust. In parks he sits on a plaster bench, discussing problems with Lenin. His picture in needle work is undertaken by the students of schools. The stores sell millions and millions of his face, and every house has at least one picture of him. Surely the painting and modeling, the casting, the forging, and the embroidering of Stalin must be one of the great industries of the Soviet Union. He is everywhere, he sees everything.

To Americans, with their fear and hatred of power invested in one man, and of perpetuation of power, this is a frightening thing and a distasteful one. At public celebrations the pictures of Stalin outgrow every bound of reason. They may be eight stories high and fifty feet wide. Every public building carries monster portraits of him.

We spoke of this to a number of Russians and had several answers. One was that the Russian people had been used to pictures of the czar and the czar's family, and when the czar was removed they needed something to substitute for him. Another was that the icon is a Russian habit of mind, and this was a kind of an icon. A third, that the Russians love Stalin so much that they want him ever present. A fourth, that Stalin himself does not like this and has asked that it be discontinued. But it seems to us that Stalin's dislike for anything else causes its removal, but this is on the increase. Whatever the reason is, one spends no moment except under the smiling, or pensive, or stern eye of Stalin. It is one of those things an American is incapable of understanding emotionally. There are other pictures and other statues too. And one can tell approximately what the succession is by the size of the photographs and portraits of other leaders in relation to Stalin. Thus in 1936, the second largest picture to Stalin's was of Voroshilov, and now the second largest picture is invariably Molotov.

—*John Steinbeck:*
A Russian Journal

ror of Stalin's guard and the puzzlement of the yardmen, who couldn't figure out whether it was the great leader himself or the actor Gelovani. Stalin apparently wanted Dovzhenko to make a romantic, heroic film similar to *Shchors* about his own contributions to the Civil War. Alas, Dovzhenko failed to understand the Master's transparent hints; he didn't make the film the leader expected of him and paid for it. Subsequently his films were either cut to shreds by the censor, or not released at all.

In 1940 a series of medals was to be awarded to a group of filmmakers. However, to the keen disappointment of the directors who expected to receive them, Stalin happened to see the film *The Great Waltz,* which had just been brought in from the Polish territory annexed under the Molotov-Ribbentrop Pact. Stalin crossed out the entire list of films presented to him for his approval. "When they learn to work like the Americans," he said, "then they'll get their medals."

OPPOSITE: *Sports demonstration on Red Square, 1936; the text on the building reads, "Ardent Greetings to the Best Friend of Sportsmen—Comrade Stalin." The formation of demonstrators on the Square spells out "Stalin."*

How simple-minded I was! I did not realize how much depended on the tastes, and even on the mood, of one man. But even those who were well aware of this could not foresee what would happen on the morrow.

While I was in Moscow Stalin made the statement: "Mayakovsky was and remains the best, the most talented poet of our Soviet epoch." Immediately everybody started to talk about the importance of innovation, of new forms, of breaking away from routine.

Some months later I read an article in *Pravda* called "Muddle Instead of Music":

Stalin had been to hear Shostakovich's opera *Katerina Izmailova* and the music had made him angry. Composers and musicians were hastily convened and they convicted Shostakovich of "clowning" and even of "cynicism."

From music they passed on with ease to literature, painting, the theater, the cinema. The critics demanded "simplicity and popular appeal." They still continued to praise Mayakovsky, of course, but in a different way now: he was "simple and close to the people."

—*Ilya Ehrenburg:* Memoirs 1921-1941

Suddenly everyone rose and began to clap furiously: entering from a side door, which I could not see, Stalin appeared followed by the members of the Politburo—I had met them at Gorky's *dacha*. The audience clapped and shouted. This went on for a long time, possibly ten or fifteen minutes. Stalin clapped in response. When the applause began to die down someone shouted: "Hurrah for the great Stalin!" and it started up all over again. At last everyone sat down and then a woman's wild cry went up: "Glory to Stalin!" We jumped to our feet and started clapping once more.

By the time this came to an end, my palms positively hurt. I was seeing Stalin for the first time and could not take my eyes off him. I knew him from hundreds of portraits, knew his tunic and his moustache, but I had imagined him taller. His hair was very black, his forehead low, his eyes keen and expressive. At times, leaning to the right or left, he smiled, at others he sat motionless though his eyes continued to gleam brightly. I found that I was hardly listening; I was so intent on watching Stalin. Turning round I saw that everybody else was doing the same.

On the way home I felt uneasy. Of course Stalin was a great man, but he was a Communist, a Marxist; we talked a lot about a new culture, but behaved not unlike the shaman whom I had seen in Upper Shoria....

At the conference Stalin had said: "People must be tended carefully and lovingly, as a gardener tends a favorite fruit-tree." These words inspired everyone: after all, they were human beings, not robots, who were sitting in the Kremlin, and they rejoiced at the thought that they would be treated carefully and lovingly....

—*Ilya Ehrenburg:* **Memoirs 1921-1941**

As for the presents which were sent to him from all corners of the earth (after the Nineteenth Party Congress in October, 1952, he twice informed the Central Committee that he wished to retire; it was probably because he was ill; in any case the fact that he wanted to retire is known to everyone who belonged to the Central Committee at that time), he had them collected in one spot and donated to a museum. It wasn't hypocrisy or a pose on his part, as a lot of people say, but simply the fact that he had no idea what to do with this avalanche of objects that were valuable, sometimes priceless: paintings, china, furniture, weapons, clothing, utensils and products of local craftsmanship from everywhere in the world.

Once in a while he gave one of them, a Rumanian or Bulgarian folk costume or something like that, to me. On the whole, however, he considered it wrong that any personal use should be made even of the things that were sent to me. Maybe he realized that the feelings that went into them were symbolic, and he thought the things themselves deserved to be treated as symbols.

In 1950 a Museum of Gifts was opened in Moscow.

—Svetlana Alliluyeva:
Twenty Letters to a Friend

OPPOSITE: *Commemorative plate portraits of the young Stalin (ca. 1900), and Stalin the Generalissimo, post-1945; USSR Museum of the Revolution, Moscow.*
ABOVE: *Tapestry depicting Lenin and Stalin; the smaller portraits and pictures around the border show the young Lenin and various revolutionaries and historical locations.*
RIGHT: *Patchwork banner depicting the various nationalities of the USSR; the banner reads, "Long Live the Brotherly Union of the Peoples of the USSR!"; gift to Stalin from the "Udarnik" Factory in Kuibyshev region, USSR Museum of the Revolution.*

Several months ago I had occasion to visit the institutes where artists, all working for the government, were engaged in their work. I found that practically all of the more noteworthy artists were employed in painting large murals for this twentieth anniversary of the Revolution, for the Red Army celebration, and for various government institutions. These paintings were evident in great profusion here. Huge lithographic mural oil paintings depicting historic scenes of the Revolution and portraits of the various government leaders were displayed attached to the sides of the buildings, and some of them were of a size of at least 30 by 20 feet. These were generally illumined at night by indirect lighting. These oil paintings were supplemented by innumerable lithographic posters, not printed but done in crayon either in colors or in black and white.

As heretofore stated, there were also large plaster statues of Lenin and Stalin both in white and in bronze. On the corner façade of one of the prominent buildings in the center of Moscow there was suspended above the street level a huge statue of Lenin attached to the side of the building and measuring at least 30 feet in height.

—*Joseph E. Davies:* Mission to Moscow

OPPOSITE: *Painting of the Awarding of the Order of Lenin to the city of Moscow on the occasion of its 800th anniversary. This monumental painting was the work of a team of artists; Stalin himself is not present, but his white marble bust dominates the entire scene.*
ABOVE: *Stalin with a map of Russia showing forest planting for soil-erosion prevention; USSR Museum of the Revolution.*
BELOW: *Portrait of Stalin with traditional Armenian decorative border; USSR Museum of the Revolution.*

We live, deaf to the land beneath us,
Ten steps away no one hears our speeches,

But where there's so much as half a conversation
The Kremlin's mountaineer will get his mention.

His fingers are fat as grubs
And the words, final as lead weights, fall from his lips,

His cockroach whiskers leer
And his boot tops gleam.

Around him a rabble of thin-necked leaders—
fawning half-men for him to play with.

They whinny, purr or whine
As he prates and points a finger,

One by one forging his laws, to be flung
Like horseshoes at the head, the eye or the groin.

And every killing is a treat
For the broad-chested Ossete.

—Osip Mandelstam, 1933
translated by Max Hayward; from
Hope Against Hope by Nadezhda Mandelstam

The Inner Circle

After working in the Kremlin two years, Ganshin was invited to join the Ninth Section of the Special Sector of the Kremlin Guard. The initiated knew that the Ninth Section was exclusively devoted to guarding Stalin. The authorities were pleased with Ganshin's work; he had good recommendations, he would be certified, he was told. This meant that he would continue working as a projectionist, but that from now on he would also be an officer of the Kremlin Guard, of the inner circle. He would receive an NKVD uniform and the equivalent of a lieutenant's rank, and an officer's pay—twice his previous salary. And he would be given the red identification booklet of an NKVD officer, a priceless document. Ganshin had no desire to arrest anyone himself (his job didn't require it, and he never showed any personal initiative in this respect), but now he could rest easy for his family. If anyone gave him trouble, they'd back off as soon as they saw his little red book.

OPPOSITE: *Stalin leaving his official limousine on his way to the Tushino Aerodrome for the celebration of Air Force Day, 1950. Note the thickness of the bulletproof doors; this car was said to have weighed about nine tons.*

The certification meant that Ganshin was trusted completely. He had always felt a little bit uncomfortable at work because a guy named Voronkov, an NKVD man, was posted next to him in the projectionist's booth. The guy didn't know anything about films, but he watched Ganshin like a hawk. Ganshin's first day on the job, Voronkov kept a suspicious eye on the toothbrush he used to clean the frame holder. Maybe he thought it was some kind of diabolical weapon. Now they wouldn't bother him with such trifles.

Though Ganshin was only supposed to wear the officer's uniform on special occasions, his new position did bring increased obligations. He had to stay in shape, do calisthenics every day, and study martial arts. He also had to learn to use a gun and practice target shooting regularly. Though he was only a projectionist, he was still a member of Stalin's guard; you never knew when you might have to use your skills, on or off duty.

The commandant of the Ninth Section, Nikolai Vlasik, knew every person who was allowed to come into direct contact with Stalin. He personally picked each of them, checked them, and rechecked them. He had to be absolutely certain that these people were trustworthy. There were, of course, mishaps. Like the young waitress. According to the rules of Kremlin service, whenever a member of the Politburo walked down the hall, you were supposed to stand with your back to the wall and hands at your sides. The waitress was new, and unfortunately for her, she happened to be holding a tray when Molotov passed by with a member of the guard one day. She stood with her back to the wall and then, when Molotov had already gone by, suddenly remembered that her hands were supposed to be at her sides. The tray and the dishes clattered to the floor. The guard turned and shot at

the sound before he realized what had happened. The fellow had been well trained, and he didn't miss.

There were thirty-four people in Stalin's guard. Three eight-hour shifts of nine people each provided round-the-clock protection for Stalin. Every shift included a chauffeur, the chauffeur's guard, and three members of the inner guard—those who were "attached" to Stalin, who were required never to let him out of their sight. This was a particularly responsible post—you had to be ready to fulfill

---

I must now mention another general, Nikolai Vlasik, who was first assigned to my father by the Red Army as a bodyguard in 1919 and remained with him for a very long time, finally attaining immense power behind the scenes. He was in charge of all my father's security arrangements and considered himself closer to my father than anybody else. And though he was incredibly stupid, illiterate and uncouth, he behaved like a grandee and took it on himself in my father's last years to dictate "Comrade Stalin's tastes," which he thought he knew well, to various luminaries in the arts. And they had to listen and take his advice. No Bolshoi gala performance on the eve of November 7 or state banquet in St. George's Hall of the Kremlin was allowed to take place without Vlasik's passing on the program first. His insolence knew no bounds. He would graciously pass the word to people in the arts whether this or that movie or opera or even the shapes of the skyscrapers being built in those days had found favor or not with my father.

He did a lot to spoil our lives and wouldn't be worth mentioning at all except that he was the kind of colorful personality you can't ignore. As far as the household staff was concerned, the name "Vlasik" was nearly as important as that of my father himself. My father, after all, was way up there on his pinnacle, and it was in Vlasik's power to do anything he liked. While my mother was alive he remained somewhere in the background as a member of my father's bodyguard and never set foot in the house. Later, however, he was a permanent fixture of the household at Kuntsevo. From there he ran all my father's other residences, which became more and more numerous as the years went by....

The rooms were the same and had the same furniture and there were exactly the same flowers and bushes outside the house. Vlasik would give the word as to what "the boss" did or didn't like. My father seldom visited either place, sometimes not for a year at a time, but the staff always expected him at any moment and was in a perpetual state of readiness. And if a motorcade actually did take off from Kuntsevo in the direction of Lipki, pandemonium would break loose there and everyone from the cook to the guard at the gate, from the waitresses to the commandant, would be seized by panic. They all awaited these visitations like Judgement Day, but the one they were most frightened of was the crude martinet Vlasik, who loved shouting at them and giving them all hell.

Svetlana Alliluyeva:
Twenty Letters to a Friend

Stalin's orders immediately, at any moment. There were also at least four messengers— sometimes as many as nine—ready to act as couriers and run other errands. The "inner circle" of people who were allowed to come into direct contact with Stalin also included his personal doctors (three of them: a senior doctor and his assistants), four cooks, gardeners, maids, and the housekeeper, who supervised them all.

Sometimes Ganshin would have to stand in for one of the guards who accompanied Stalin in his car. Stalin would usually sit on the jump seat. Two guards would cover him from each side, and a third from the front, next to the driver. Once Ganshin saw Vlasik showing Stalin the new car that had been made for him. Stalin took Vlasik's pistol and fired at the door. He was pleased with the result: The bullet only slightly dented the steel plate but didn't penetrate it. Ganshin saw that Stalin was very careful. But what was he afraid of? Stalin himself feared nothing, Ganshin thought, but he had to think about the country, about the people. What would happen to them if our enemies managed to do away with Stalin?

Stalin lived in constant expectation of an assassination attempt. He was afraid of being poisoned: All the food sent to his kitchen was sealed and accompanied by a special affidavit from a toxicologist, certifying its purity. But this did not entirely assuage his fear. Whenever any dish attracted his attention at the table, he would first ask one of his guests to try it. He feared that poisons might be carried through the air, so a special doctor periodically checked and certified the air in his Kremlin apartment.

He was also afraid of a guerrilla attack, and this fear increased with the years. Before 1931 he would still travel and walk through the city without his bodyguards. Later, the guard never left his side even within the Kremlin walls. Lenin's personal guard had consisted of two people; after Fanny Kaplan's attempt on Lenin's life, his guard was increased to four. In comparison, Stalin's guard, in addition to the "inner circle," constituted an entire army. The "near" *dacha*, or summer house, in Kuntsevo on the outskirts of Moscow, was under round-the-clock observation by hundreds of agents and was protected by a hidden barbed-wire fence that was electrified. The route from Stalin's *dacha* to the Kremlin was guarded twenty-four hours a day (in three shifts) by NKVD agents. Every shift consisted of about 1200 men.

And even this, it appears, wasn't enough. Three-quarters of the people living on the street Stalin traveled on his way to the *dacha* were evicted, and NKVD agents and their families were settled in their places. For greater security, Stalin would frequently change his route at the very last minute. His car was armored, of course, and the window glass was three centimeters thick. When he appeared on the mausoleum tribune on state holidays, Stalin wore a bulletproof vest, custom-made for him in Germany, underneath his uniform. For trips to his "southern" *dacha*, Stalin had a special armored train outfitted with shutters that would automatically close if the alarm were sounded. The train was equipped to withstand a two-week siege.

The greater Stalin's fear grew, the more important became the role of the chief of the Kremlin guard. General-Lieutenant Vlasik was the longest-lasting of Stalin's guard chiefs. He was extremely loyal to Stalin, was virtually in charge of raising the leader's children, and followed his every order. He is said to have disobeyed him only once. It occurred during a German air attack when two bombs fell on the territory of the Kremlin. Stalin threw on his overcoat so he could go outside to see what had happened. Vlasik blocked the doorway and refused to let him pass. "You don't work for me anymore," said Stalin. Vlasik was prepared to accept this. The next morning Stalin's anger had changed to affection. Vlasik stayed on....

From the moment he began working in the Kremlin, Ganshin felt himself to be part of a very special world, a world totally unlike the one that existed outside the Kremlin's crenelated walls. Here everything was ideally clean, everything was in perfect order. All the food in the cafeteria was fresh as could be. Fresh, soft rolls, cold kefir, snow-white sour cream. All the relations between people were regulated, and it wasn't a good idea to test the limits.

On becoming an officer of the Ninth Section, Ganshin became even more aware of how well the Kremlin mechanism worked. Members of the Ninth Section were not allowed to be "exposed" in the photographs that were taken in great quantities for the press on all official occasions where Stalin was present. You had to learn the difficult trick of staying close to Stalin all the time, but becoming invisible just when the shutter clicked. Those who broke the rules twice were fired without any discussion.

Making any personal appeals was strictly forbidden, although many of the people who worked for Stalin or for members of the Politburo lived in extremely poor circumstances. They were instructed to answer any question about their living conditions with the answer: "Everything's fine, Comrade Stalin, I have no complaints." "Everything's fine, Comrade Molotov, no complaints." But it was hard to resist the temptation to ask for an apartment or at least a room—they all suffered cramped living quarters. A few did receive an apartment in the end, but they didn't keep their jobs. Stalin would haul Vlasik over the coals for not taking care of his people, and Vlasik would take it out on the petitioner.

An even more serious crime was to try to give personal letters to Stalin. A great many people wanted to appeal to the leader. After all, Stalin could do anything, he had the power to help anyone out of a difficult spot. But Stalin never forgave even his beloved daughter Svetlana for attempts to play "mailman."

After he became a member of the inner circle, Ganshin's trips to Stalin's *dacha* just outside Moscow grew more frequent. Ganshin had been there before, but now he would sometimes spend the night after a screening. Once he was called to the *dacha*, but when he got there he found out he was urgently needed back at the Kremlin. No car was available, so Svetlana drove him on her motorcycle. She was sixteen years old at the time, and raced along the roads at high speed, paying no attention to traffic lights or to the policemen, who stood at attention and saluted her as she zoomed past. On that trip into the Kremlin Ganshin got such a scare that he refused to ride with her again.

Ganshin was well liked by the people who worked with him: He was friendly and easygoing. Once he was called to show a film at a birthday party for Stalin's son Vasily. By the time he got there the festivities were well under way, the "birthday boy" had had quite a bit to drink, and it seemed Ganshin wouldn't be showing any films that night. But his presence proved useful nonetheless. The record player broke, and he was asked to fix it. Ganshin was good with machines and quickly located the problem, but to impress them with his importance and knowledge he took longer

than necessary to fix it. Vasily poured him a glass of cognac by way of thanks, and since Ganshin rarely drank, it went straight to his head. He dozed off on his chair. They set up a screen around him so he could sleep, and continued the party. Ganshin woke up abruptly, startled by the sudden silence. The guests had disappeared and there were only two other people in the room: Stalin and his son. They were sitting at the table, talking. Behind his screen, Ganshin was stiff with fear. He couldn't let himself be known. God forbid Stalin should think that he was eavesdropping!

In America there are many hundreds of houses where George Washington slept, and in Russia there are many places where Joseph Stalin worked. The railroad shops in Tiflis have against their outer wall a bank of flowers and a giant plaque proclaiming that in this shop Joseph Stalin once had a job. Stalin is a Georgian by birth, and his birthplace, Gori, about seventy kilometers from Tiflis, has already become a national shrine....

The birthplace of Stalin has been left as it was, and whole thing covered by an enormous canopy to protect it from the weather. The top of the canopy is of stained glass. The birthplace is a tiny one-story house, built of plaster and rubble, a house of two rooms with a little porch that runs along the front. And even so, the family of Stalin were so poor that they only lived in half of the house, in one room. There is a rope across the door, but one can look inside at the bed, the shallow clothes closet, a little table, a samovar, and a crooked lamp. And in this room the family lived, and cooked, and slept. Square golden marble columns support the canopy of stained glass. And this structure is set in a large rose garden. On the edge of the rose garden there is the museum of Stalin, in which is preserved every article that could be gathered that is associated with his childhood and early manhood— early photographs and paintings of everything that he did....

In all history we could not think of anyone so honored in his lifetime. We can only think of Augustus Caesar in this respect, and we doubt whether even Augustus Caesar had during his lifetime the prestige, the veneration, and the god-like hold on his people that Stalin has. What Stalin says is true to them, even if it seems to be contrary to natural law....

If Stalin can have this amount of power during his lifetime, what will he become when he is dead? In many speeches in Russia we have heard the speaker suddenly quote a line from a speech of Stalin's that has the stopping quality of the *ipse dixit* of the medieval scholar who put his argument in the lap of Aristotle. In Russia there is no appeal from the word of Stalin, and there is no argument against anything he says. And however this has been accomplished, by propaganda, by training, by constant reference, by the iconography which is ever present, it is nevertheless true. And you can only get the sense of this force when you hear, as we did many times, the remark, "Stalin has never been wrong. In his whole life he has not been wrong once." And the man who says it does not offer it as an argument, it is not refutable, he says it as a matter completely true and beyond argument.

—*John Steinbeck:* A Russian Journal

He wouldn't stand on ceremony—Ganshin knew that much.

He heard Stalin drum his fingers on the table in irritation. Then the leader said to his son, "All you do is drink and have a good time. You've stopped studying. You think you know everything! And here I am, an old man, and I'm still studying.... And every day I realize more and more how much I still have to learn!" And he left the room....

Today, Ganshin is irked by talk of the "bad" Stalin, and of the "cult of personality" that the

OPPOSITE: *Stalin's mother, Ekaterina Geladze Dzhugashvili.*
LEFT: *Stalin's second wife, Nadezhda Alliluyeva, with the infant Svetlana, 1920s.*
ABOVE: *Left to right: Vasily Stalin, Andrei Zhdanov, Svetlana, Stalin, and Yakov Dzhugashvili (Stalin's son by his first marriage) at the* dacha, *ca. mid-1930s.*

leader imposed on the country. Other people started the cult, he thinks, and made a big thing of it, and then they went and blamed everything on Stalin. He could tell you a lot of stories, he says (some he witnessed himself, others he heard about from his friends in the Kremlin Guard), that testify to Stalin's humility, his concern for others, his respect for other people. Once, at a banquet, for instance, when the toasts were just about to start, Stalin was the first to lift his glass: "Let's drink to the great leader and teacher of all peoples, Comrade Stalin," said the Master, "and then let's forget about that." That shut up all those hangers-on.

Or there was the time when Stalin went to his *dacha* in the Caucasus for medical treatment. Mzhavanadze, a Georgian Communist Party functionary, met him at the station and began speaking Georgian. Stalin immediately cut the conversation short: "Speak Russian," he said. "I don't understand Georgian."

Stalin, a Georgian himself, said that out of respect for his guard: It isn't polite to speak a language others don't understand.

When Stalin died, his housekeeper of eighteen years, Valentina Istomina, fell on her knees next to the sofa where he lay, flung herself over his chest, and wept like a peasant woman. All in all, Stalin's relations with his inner circle were apparently warmer and more human than with any of his closest associates in the Politburo. Stalin knew almost all his guards by name; he would inquire after their

health and the well-being of their families. He liked to attend amateur concerts put on by the members of his guard, and Vlasik, knowing the Master's tastes, was good at arranging these performances. There were fellows among them who knew how to sing, dance, and play instruments—and it was flattering to perform for such an audience.

Ganshin didn't often have direct contact with Stalin. He sat in the projection booth and Stalin and the members of the Politburo sat in the screening room. They really weren't visi-

ble through the window of the booth, except when one of them got up to walk around. Ganshin went into the screening room only on those rare occasions when, because of some technical problem, he was sent to tell the Master that everything had been fixed, everything was fine, and the viewing could be continued. Sometimes Stalin praised him: "Good going! You did a quick job. We haven't even had time to finish a cup of tea, and you've already fixed the problem." Or he'd say, "What's the problem? Did the machine go bad on you? Maybe you haven't been taking good enough care of it." "No," replied Ganshin, unflustered, "I take good care of it. But anything can happen. You can court a woman day and night, but you can never tell what she'll do next." The leader and his associates liked this answer, and they all laughed.

All of the guard thought of Stalin not only as a god, but also as a kind, warm human being. They feared him, but they loved him. Ganshin knew both Stalin the god, the public image on the posters and monuments, and the terrestrial Stalin, the simple human being who liked to work in the garden. The two Stalins merged in his consciousness, and his belief in the one never interfered with his belief in the other.

OPPOSITE: *Stalin with Svetlana, early 1930s.*
ABOVE: *Stalin carrying Svetlana back to the* **dacha,** *1935.*
BELOW: *Stalin and Svetlana, 1935.*

The Terror Spreads

Even today, Ganshin and many people like him don't question the correctness of Stalin's policies. The country had to be industrialized, didn't it? Otherwise the Germans would have won the war! And if there were some "excesses" in the process, what can you do? Stalin was right to put an end to the private enterprise of NEP (New Economic Policy), which Lenin had begun in the 1920s, when the economy had nearly come to a halt. People were getting too rich, all at the expense of the working class! Stalin was right to shake them down. That's what the Revolution had been for, Ganshin thought: to make everyone equal. And the collectivization of agriculture that began in the late 1920s—there, too, Stalin was right to force the peasants off the land and into collective farms.

Rather than argue with Ganshin, let us simply stop for a moment and think about what he refused to think about, or perhaps didn't know: the price the country and the people paid for these policies.

The peasants stubbornly resisted collectivization. On the collective farm they were no longer masters of their own land, the very land for which they had supported the Bolsheviks and helped them win the Revolution. The government now took their grain from them at a price that often did not even permit them to feed their families, much less buy clothes and shoes. But Stalin understood the situation very well. In a country where two-thirds of the population was rural, independent farmers posed a threat to the government's power and control. It was important to break the peasantry's back.

In the beginning of the 1930s a system of internal passports and residence permits was introduced in the USSR; the system still exists today. A person had the right to live only at the address written in his or her passport. You had to get special permission to move to another house or apartment (and the housing shortage made this almost impossible anyway), or to another city. People's mobility was severely limited. But the situation of the collective farm workers was even worse. They had no passports at all. They were registered at their collective farm and did not have the right to leave it.

Becoming a member of a collective farm

OPPOSITE: *Peasants "voting" to join the* kolkhoz *(collective farm), 1929. Millions of peasants were killed during the forced collectivization of agriculture, and the country has yet to recover from the disastrous effects of these policies.*

was supposed to be voluntary, but in fact people were often impressed into service. Collectivization was accompanied by a widespread campaign of terror. The government began a war against "kulaks," independent peasant farmers. Anyone who worked hard and had managed to save a bit extra for another cow or horse, or to build a house or buy time-saving equipment, could be considered a kulak. Entire families were forcibly resettled in uninhabited regions of Siberia and the North, where they had to start over again in an inhospitable climate with nothing but their bare hands. Many died along the way, and many were shot for attempts to resist. The number of people who died one way or another as a result of collectivization and "dekulakization" is difficult to determine; historians give figures ranging from nine million to twenty-five million.

Peasant resistance to collectivization took different forms. Sometimes they killed off cattle: By 1933 the head count was two to three times lower than it had been at the end of the 1920s before collectivization. There was some armed resistance, and at times it was so desperate that the army was brought in. The vanquished were treated without mercy. For that matter, the resisters could be just as harsh themselves, on the few occasions when they had the upper hand: In the North Caucasus, for instance, the Cossacks surrounded and killed an entire regiment. Hundreds of corpses floated down the rivers of the region.

Another result of collectivization was famine in the fertile lands of the Ukraine, Kuban, and

ABOVE: *Peasant woman feeding her child in a field, Byelorussia, 1923.*
OPPOSITE: *Propaganda poster directed at peasants; "Not One Acre Left Unreaped!", 1931.*

the Volga region in the early 1930s. This famine was not brought on by a bad harvest or war, it was organized by the authorities. Stalin was settling accounts with the peasants who would not bend to his will. Entire villages died out. To make sure that people couldn't escape to the city, roads were cut off by detachments of NKVD troops. Officially, the famine didn't exist: It was never mentioned in a single Soviet paper. But the unofficial figures now available suggest from five million to eight million people died.

On August 7, 1932, a law on "the safekeeping of socialist property" was passed. Stalin personally added these words: "People who encroach upon socialist property should be considered enemies of the people." Those were terrifying words, "enemies of the people." You could be shot for that. The age limit for the death penalty was reduced to twelve: Even young boys and girls were shot for collecting ears of wheat left over in the fields after the harvest had been gathered. At the very least, you got ten years in a prison camp for this crime. No amnesty was allowed. Less than five months after this law had been passed, 54,645 people had been sentenced under it; 2,110 received the death penalty.

Here are some examples of the sentences given under the "law of the wheat ears," as it was called among the people: A soldier's widow and her two neighbors were each given two years for collecting half a sack of frozen beets from an abandoned collective farm field near Poltavshchina. Rogozhin, an inhabitant of the Omsk region, was given five years in a prison

BELOW: *Building the Turkistan-Siberian railway, 1928. These Central Asian riders hold a portrait of Stalin and a makeshift sign reading "We will sharply repulse the Self-Seekers and Wreckers of Production."*

camp for "hoarding foodstuffs"—he was found to have half a sack of flour and several kilos of butter and honey. Two women from a village near Chita were each condemned to five years in prison for bartering tobacco for bread at a market.

Soviet agriculture has not yet recovered from the damage done by collectivization. Many villages died out or were abandoned. The people who best knew how to work the land were systematically destroyed. Though things were better in the cities, conditions were still far from the minimum living conditions taken for granted in other European countries; goods were rationed or in short supply.

Ganshin worked hard. He often returned home only after three in the morning. His wife worried that his health would suffer. She often said, "Let's leave it all. We'll go to the countryside, to my parents. I can't stand to see you work so hard." But Ganshin knew that there was nothing for them in the countryside. And he had a daughter now. What would she do there? Here in Moscow he had a good job and plenty of money. And even if he wanted to leave, they wouldn't let him go. Working for the Ninth Section was serious business.

Ganshin and others like him were utterly convinced that they knew what the problem was: Living conditions in the whole country would be a lot better even now if it weren't for wreckers and saboteurs. In virtually every new film Ganshin showed Stalin, spies and wreckers were caught or uncovered. They were either kulaks in disguise who had craftily stolen a Party membership card from some heroine who had lost her class instinct, or agents sent from abroad, or bourgeois specialists who pretended to support Soviet power

We never asked, on hearing about the latest arrest, "What was he arrested for?" but we were exceptional. Most people, crazed by fear, asked this question just to give themselves a little hope: if others were arrested for some reason, then they wouldn't be arrested, because they hadn't done anything wrong. They vied with each other in thinking up ingenious reasons to justify each arrest: "Well, she really is a smuggler, you know," "He really did go rather far," "I myself heard him say..." Or: "It was only to be expected—he's a terrible man," "I always thought there was something fishy about him," "He isn't one of us at all." This was enough for anyone to be arrested and destroyed: "not one of us," "talks too much," "a bad character"...These were just variations on a theme we had first heard in 1917. Both public opinion and the police kept inventing new and more graphic ones, adding fuel to the fire without which there is no smoke. This was why we had outlawed the question "What was he arrested for?" "*What for?*" Akhmatova would cry indignantly whenever, infected by the prevailing climate, anyone of our circle asked this question. "What do you mean, *what for*? It's time you understood that people are arrested *for nothing!*..."

We were constantly forced by the circumstances of our life to behave like members of a secret society. When we met we spoke in whispers, glancing at the walls for fear of eavesdropping neighbors or hidden microphones. When I returned to Moscow after the war, I found that everybody covered their telephones with cushions, because it was rumored that they were equipped with recording devices....Nobody trusted anyone else, and every acquaintance was a suspected police informer. It sometimes seemed as though the whole country was suffering from persecution mania, and we still haven't recovered from it.

—*Nadezhda Mandelstam:*
Hope Against Hope

There had been a time when, terrified of chaos, we had all prayed for a strong system, for a powerful hand that would stem the angry human river overflowing its banks. This fear of chaos is perhaps the most permanent of our feelings—we have still not recovered from it, and it is passed on from one generation to another. There is not one of us—either among the old who saw the Revolution or the young and innocent—who does not believe that he would be the first victim if ever the mob got out of hand. "We should be the first to be hanged from a lamppost"—whenever I hear this constantly repeated phrase, I remember Herzen's words about the intelligentsia which so much fears its own people that it prefers to go in chains itself, provided the people, too, remain fettered.

What we wanted was for the course of history to be made smooth, all the ruts and potholes to be removed, so there should never again be any unforeseen events and everything should flow along evenly and according to plan. This longing prepared us, psychologically, for the appearance of the Wise Leaders who would tell us where we were going. And once they were there, we no longer ventured to act without their guidance and looked to them for direct instructions and foolproof prescriptions. Since we could offer no better prescriptions of our own, it was logical to accept the ones proposed from on high. The most we dared do was offer advice in some minor matter: would it be possible, for example, to allow different styles in carrying out the Party's orders in art? We would like it so much....In our blindness we ourselves struggled to impose unanimity—because in every disagreement, in every difference of opinion, we saw the beginnings of new anarchy and chaos. And either by silence or consent we ourselves helped the system to gain in strength and protect itself against its detractors—such as the housekeeper in Cherdyn, or various poets and chatterboxes.

—*Nadezhda Mandelstam:*
Hope Against Hope

but were really planning all kinds of villainy. It seemed that the more the Soviet people achieved, the greater the number of enemies and wreckers were uncovered. Comrade Stalin explained this to the people: The closer we get to achieving our goals, the closer we are to the final victory of communism, the more vehement the resistance of our enemies.

No one will ever know whether Stalin actually believed in this theory, whether he truly imagined enemies and wreckers everywhere, or whether this was a conscious ploy invented as an excuse to unleash a wave of terror and thereby subjugate the entire country. In any event, by September 1930

OPPOSITE, TOP: *Children carrying a banner reading, "Down with Religious Holidays. Long Live Socialist Competition and Shockwork in the Forest!", Verkhny Udai, Eastern Siberian region, 1931.*

OPPOSITE, BOTTOM: *Demonstrators on Red Square, Moscow, 1930s. The banner reads, "Severely Judge the Right-wing Renegades, Betrayers and Traitors to the Motherland."*

FOLLOWING PAGE: LEFT: *Meeting of workers at the S.M. Kirov Factory, Leningrad, 1938. The slogan reads, "Death to the Fascist Dogs! The Fascists Will Never Set Foot on Sacred Soviet Land!"* RIGHT, TOP: *Workers "voting" at a meeting, "Dinamo" Factory, 1936. The banner says, "Wipe the Trotsky-Zinovyevite gang of murderers from the face of the Earth—Such is the Verdict of the Working People!"* RIGHT, BOTTOM: *Factory workers at a meeting; the sign in the background reads, "Death to the Whole Trotskyite [Band]!", 1930s.*

Стереть с лица земли троцкистско-зиновьевскую банду убийц - таков приговор трудового народа!

Смерть отец троцкизм

Stalin knew precisely on whom to lay the blame for the shortages of goods. In a letter to Molotov recently unearthed in state archives, Stalin wrote: "Vyacheslav! We should immediately publish all the evidence on meat, fish, canned food, and vegetable saboteurs and then a week later have the OGPU announce that all the scoundrels have been shot. They should all be shot."

There had been no investigation, no trial, no one had established the guilt of those arrested. Stalin had said they were guilty, and that was enough to condemn them to death.

Soon wreckers were uncovered in all spheres of society: in transportation and energy, in the oil fields and the mines, in textile and machine factories, in the chemical industry and irrigation, in the universities and hospitals, in the Army and the Navy. Everything could be explained in this way: Why there were no clothes on sale in the stores, nothing to eat. Why there was chaos in transportation. Why apartments were poorly heated in winter. …It was the "wreckers," as the investigations of the NKVD showed, members of the classes overthrown by the Revolution: the children of

capitalists, landowners, kulaks, and the clergy. They were representatives of the old intelligentsia—engineers, professors, economists, and military specialists. They hated the new order and dreamed of restoring the old ways. Show trials were organized, like the famous Shakhty Case against engineers in 1928. At these trials, the accused seemed to compete with each other to reveal their crimes. They "confessed" to organizing famines and founding opposition parties and conspiratorial groups, and to being the paid agents of world imperialism. In the 1930s they increasingly "confessed" to planning the assassination of Stalin, Kirov, Gorky, and Ordzhonikidze.

Millions of people working in factories universities, and military units demanded merciless punishment for the enemies of the people and death to traitors of the Motherland at orga-

BELOW: *Newspaper headlines: A. "We Will Be Merciless to Enemies" B. "Foul Betrayers Should Be Shot!" C. "Shoot the Bandits!" D. "No Mercy For Traitors Of The Motherland!"*

БУДЕМ БЕСПОЩАДНЫ РАГАМ

A.

ГНУСНЫХ ПРЕДАТЕЛЕЙ—РАССТРЕЛЯТЬ!

(Резолюция собрания рабочих, работниц, инженеров, техников и служащих Коломенского машиностроительного завода им. Куйбышева)

B.

Бандитов— расстрелять!

C.

НИКАКОЙ ПОЩАДЫ ИЗМЕННИКАМ РОДИНЫ!

СОВЕТСКАЯ МОЛОДЕЖЬ ВМЕСТЕ СО ВСЕМ НАРОДОМ ТРЕБУЕТ РАССТРЕЛА ПОДЛЫХ ЗАГОВОРЩИКОВ ИЗ АНТИСОВЕТСКОГО «ПРАВО-ТРОЦКИСТСКОГО БЛОКА»

D.

nized meetings. Newspaper headlines and radio programs made the same appeals. In ardent verse, poets called for vigilance—that is, for suspicion: "Comrade, remember:/ among us/ the class enemy/ is at work," the poet Vladimir Mayakovsky wrote some years before his suicide in 1930.

Until the mid-1930s, the terror generally circumvented members of the Communist Party. Membership in the Party was a kind of badge of loyalty providing protection. But midway in the decade, Party heads began rolling. These were the very people who had made the Revolution and brought Stalin to power. Some had participated in the bloody achievements of collectivization; some were people who had joined the Party simply to save their skins. The year 1937 is notable for the blow of devastating power that came down on the ruling Party itself.

For many years, Ganshin remembered the fear he felt the night they came to take him, as he thought, to Lubianka. He remembered the sleepy, frightened faces of his neighbors peeking out of their rooms,

"Black Marias," special armored vans containing individual cells, drove through the city. They were usually disguised with bright advertisements such as "Drink Tomato Juice" or signs reading "Bread" and "Meat." They brought thousands of people to the cellars of the NKVD, and most of these people disappeared without a trace. The scale of the repression is hard to grasp. During 1937–39, in Moscow alone, up to one thousand people were shot on a daily basis. (KGB officials dispute these figures, but even they have agreed on a figure of 900 executions.) Alexander Milchakov, an ex-Gulag prisoner who has investigated Stalinist crimes for many years, writes that on some nights as many as 150 trucks were brought to Lubianka to cart the corpses away.

Lubianka couldn't handle all the executions, so they were carried out in other places as well. One of them was the church of Novospassky Monastery. The prisoners thought that they were being brought to the baths. They undressed and stood up against yardsticks to have "their height measured." A little window would open in the wall behind them, and the executioner would shoot them in the back of the head. Another location was the village of Butovo, near Moscow. Trenches were dug five hundred yards long, three yards wide, and three yards deep. The condemned were brought to the edge of the pit, shot in the back of the head, and their bodies dumped in the trench. There were many such locations throughout the country.

and the same faces, even more frightened, when he returned. This fear lay deep inside everyone. Yes, people sang, "I know no other land, where man can breathe so free," and "We were born to turn fairy tales into reality"; but nonetheless, everyone was possessed by this fear. It was impossible not to know about the arrests. You could try not to think about them, and Ganshin, like many others, tried not to, or you could try to justify and explain them (enemies, wreckers, spies). But the fear could not be fully suppressed.

Today, on the basis of published documents and the memoirs of survivors, we can construct a picture of what happened at the end of the 1930s in the USSR. The reality strains the imagination. Every night "black ravens," or

ABOVE: *The accused in the "Shakhty Case" trial being brought to the court in a "black raven," or "Black Maria," Moscow, 1928. This was one of the first public "show trials."*

Untold numbers died from the overcrowding and unhygienic conditions in the jails. Zelma Belais, who spent years in prison, remembers that in her small cell in Butyrskaya Prison there were at times as many as eighty-eight people. Many died on the way to the camps in the freezing, overcrowded freight cars, where the toilet was simply a crevice in a floorboard; many died from hunger and thirst, from epidemics, and forced labor in the camps. When relatives were informed that their loved ones had been sentenced to ten years without the right to correspondence, it soon was no secret that this meant they had been shot.

Fear deprived people of sleep, and worse—it deprived them of their dignity, their conscience. You could be arrested for anything at all: for a joke, for a "bad class origin," for belonging in previous years to any other political party or opposition group within the Communist Party. You could be arrested because of your relatives, for a casual expression of dissatisfaction, for being late to work, for a factory accident, for a letter received from abroad, for a typographical error (a typist was arrested for typing "Stalin's nonsense" [*vzdor*] instead of Stalin's "gaze" [*vzor*]) or for dropping or knocking over a portrait of the Master or a bust of one of his colleagues.

The most innocent conversational remarks could result in punishment. The widow of executed Party leader Nikolai Bukharin, Anna Larina (who spent many years in a labor camp), remembers that Sarra Yakir, the widow of an executed officer, who was in the same camp with Larina, was given another ten years on top of her original sentence of eight years for remarking that the Mediterranean was no less beautiful than the Black Sea and that in Italy they made lovely embroidered blouses. This was seen as praising capitalism and thus was an act of counterrevolutionary agitation.

Denunciations flourished. People denounced one another out of fear or out of cowardice. They denounced their colleagues and neighbors to further their careers or to take over an extra room in a communal apartment. Smears and slander spread like an epidemic. Denunciations were made in and out of prison (in prison the stoolies were given extra food and privileges by the authorities). In his chronicle of the Great Terror, Robert Conquest writes, "The activity of informers grew to incredible dimensions. In Ukrainian newspapers it was announced that one inhabitant of Kiev had informed on 69 people, another on 100 people. In Odessa one Communist alone informed on 230 people. In Poltava a member of the Party 'exposed' his entire organization."

It is now estimated that one in five employees in any given Soviet organization were informants of the NKVD in one way or another. There were entire categories of workers (doormen, janitors, chauffeurs of Party members) whose very jobs required them to inform. Few people in those years managed to avoid being turned into secret informers. Another reason for this was the twelfth paragraph of the notorious Article 58 of the Criminal Code, according to which you could be imprisoned for *not* informing. Not informing was the same as committing the crime yourself. If one member of a group said something negative about Stalin and you didn't inform the proper authorities, the punishment would be the same as though you had said it yourself.

To this very day, Ganshin and other simple people like him refuse to believe that Stalin knew about the brutality in the cellars of Lubianka, about the executions without trial. However, documents that have been recently published tell the impartial truth: Stalin knew everything. Not only did he know, but he himself sanctioned the lawless-

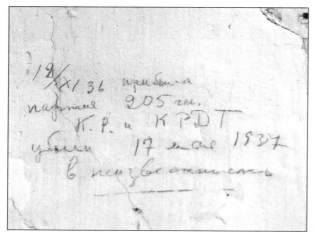

TOP: *Graffiti on the wall of a cell at Solovetsky Prison, Solovetsky Monastery, White Sea. The text reads, "On November 12, 1936, a group of 205 people, C.R.s and C.R.A.s, arrived. May 17, 1937,* THEY VANISHED INTO THE UNKNOWN." *[C.R. and C.R.A. refer to Counter-Revolution and Counter-Revolutionary Activities, the criminal articles under which these people were arrested.]*

BOTTOM: *"Common Grave No.1/ Burial place of unclaimed remains from 1930-1942"; Donskoi Monastery, Moscow. In the late 1930s, as many as 1,000 people a day were shot in the Lubianka. In 1991 this stone was replaced by a monument to the victims of Stalinism.*

OPPOSITE: *Kulaks accused of murder, 1929. Note that they are all wearing prison-issue clothing.*

ness, he was personally responsible for much of it. Stalin himself signed death sentences for individuals; he signed group sentences where the "crimes" of individuals were not even recorded. Among the death warrants with his signature are separate lists with as many as one hundred, two hundred, and three hundred names. An unusual record exists from December 12, 1938, when he and Molotov confirmed the death sentences of 3,176 people.

Besides the executions carried out "legally"—that is, with some pretense of legal decorum (official arrest, interrogation, trial)—secret executions were practiced quite frequently, and were subsequently recorded as criminal executions, automobile accidents, etc. The great Jewish actor Solomon Mikhoels was killed in this fashion; an automobile accident was staged. According to Nikita Khrushchev, the murderer received a medal for a success-fully undertaken assignment. Zinaida Raikh, the wife of the famous director Meyerhold (who had already been arrested by that time), was killed in a similar way. An employee of the NKVD climbed through her balcony window and stabbed her with a knife eight times.

The bacchanalia of executions was accompanied in public by the wise, concerned words of the leader, frequently repeated at official functions for the consumption of believers like Ganshin: "People are our most valuable capital." But Nikita Khrushchev, who knew Stalin well, had the following to say: "Stalin treated the people like a god who had created them. God thought that he had created people from clay, and what respect could you have for clay? Stalin liked to say that the people are manure. A formless mass that would follow strength." And: "The most important thing in his life," said Khrushchev, "was power—power as an end, a means, an unchanging value."

Stalin knew how to make a good impression. It was sufficient to manifest concern for a single, unknown individual, to answer just one of the thousands of letters addressed to him, for legends to spread quickly about his generosity

---

ABOVE: *Prisoners arrested in the Astrakhansky Affair in a prison excercise yard, 1929. Like the Shakhty Case, the Astrakhansky Affair was one of the early show trials; it was also directed against engineers.*

and omniscience. Stalin knew how to wear the mask of a leader, how to present himself, putting on a special face for each situation. "He acted like an open, goodhearted companion," writes Maria Ioffe, the widow of a well-known diplomat, who frequently saw Stalin at receptions and premieres. "He was extraordinarily sociable and friendly, but there was not a single drop of sincerity in any of it.... Stalin was an actor of rare talent, capable of changing his mask according to the circumstances. One of his favorite masks was that of a simple, kind fellow, unpretentious and unable to hide his emotions."

Stalin led a modest life. He liked simple food and was contemptuous of luxury and comfort. He could have lived in a magnificent historical palace inside the Kremlin walls, in an apartment with huge windows, high ceilings, and marble staircases. There were rooms in that apartment for guests, for the guard, and for receptions and servants. But Stalin almost never lived there, preferring the *dacha* in nearby Kuntsevo. According to Alexander Shelepin, a party functionary who took part in the inventory of Stalin's possessions after his death, "There were no valuable objects at the *dacha*, except for a piano. There was not even a single 'real' painting. The furniture was inexpensive. Chairs with slipcovers. No antiques. On the walls—paper reproductions in plain wood frames. The centerpiece of the room was an enlarged photograph of Lenin and Stalin. Two rugs on the floor. Stalin slept under an army blanket. Other than the marshal's uniform, the only clothes were a pair of simple suits (one of duck cloth), a pair of lined felt boots, and a peasant sheepskin coat...."

Today, in trying to understand the magic of Stalin's effect on people around him (and magic there undoubtedly was; even sophisticated visiting Western intellectuals such as Herbert Wells, George Bernard Shaw, and Romain Rolland were not immune to it), researchers see his strength not so much in any intellectual power or oratorical abilities (the utter vacuity of his speeches amazes contemporary young people), but in the feeling of absolute power that he incarnated. This power was all-encompassing. Whatever Stalin decided, that was what happened.

СЧАСТЛИВЫЕ РОДЯТСЯ ПОД СОВЕТСКОЙ ЗВЕЗДОЙ!

Thank You for Our Happy Childhood, Comrade Stalin!

Children, particularly, suffered from the crimes of the Stalin era. Soviet Pioneer Scouts swore an oath to serve "the cause of Lenin-Stalin." They were accustomed to seeing wonderful slogans such as "Thank You, Comrade Stalin, for Our Happy Childhood," and the even more wonderful portraits of a kind, fatherly Stalin greeting groups of children or holding hands with the Uzbek girl Mamlakat. They didn't know what kind of childhood the great leader had arranged for many of their peers. Even those who did not end up in the Gulag's meat grinder were forever marked by their "happy Soviet childhood." Sooner or later, the abyss

OPPOSITE: *"Happy Are Those Born Under the Soviet Star"; appliqué panel, present to Stalin from the Staro-Pavlovskaya Wool Factory.*
FOLLOWING PAGE: *Children of "Traitors to the Motherland," photographed for the registry of the special center for children of "Enemies of the People" in the St. Daniel Monastery, Moscow, 1930s. The children's names were often changed in the orphanage, but their files were kept by number, thus allowing the NKVD to keep track of the whereabouts of any given child.*

between the wonderful ideals they were taught and the real life they lived had to be revealed. You either relinquished the ability to think, came to hate the system that lied to you and taught you to lie, or cynically served the system for opportunistic purposes.

Entire families were eliminated. Frequently women who had long since divorced their husbands were arrested and sent to the camps. No special trial or permission of the prosecutor was necessary for relatives of arrested individuals to end up in the same position. It was enough to belong to one of the alphabetical groups that the creators of the Gulag invented in such quantities: ZhVN (WEP: Wife of an Enemy of the People); RVN (REP: Relative of an Enemy of the People); ChSVN (FMEP: Family Member of an Enemy of the People); ChSIR (FMTM: Family Member of a Traitor to the Motherland). These letters were enough for a camp sentence, and, if the authorities so willed, for the death penalty.

Although the munificent leader had said, "The son doesn't answer for the father," this was hardly true. All were vulnerable: children of Party officials as well as children of persecuted kulaks, noble families, and the *nouveaux* capitalists who managed to get rich during the

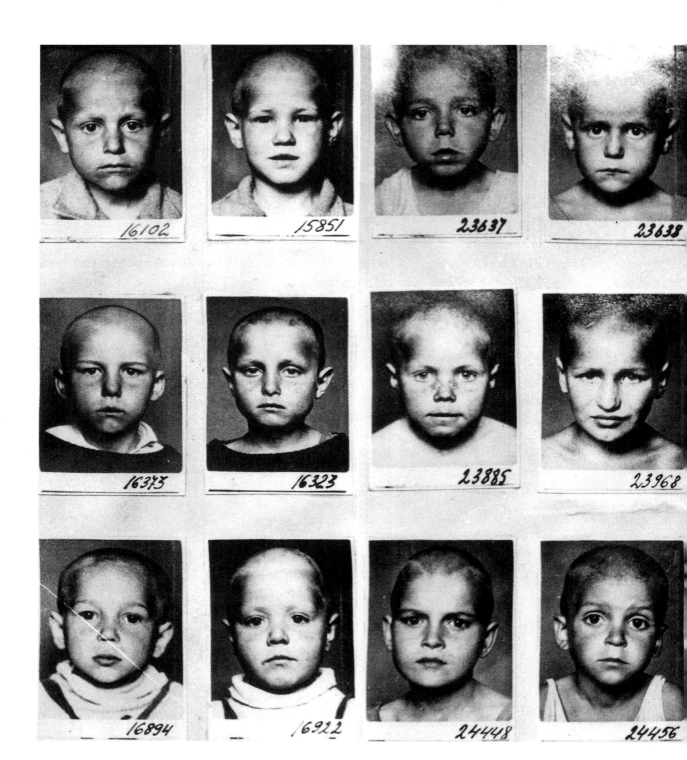

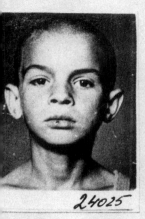
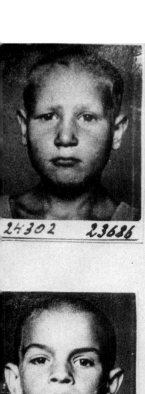
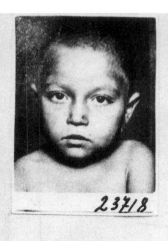
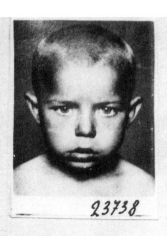
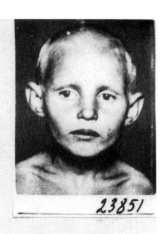

24302   23686   23718   23738   23851

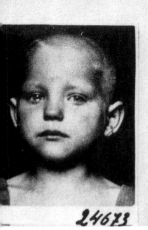
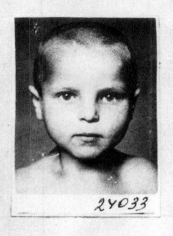
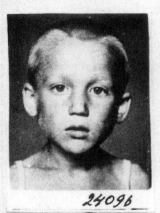
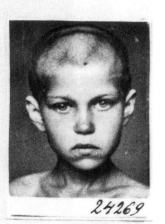

24025   24033   24096   24269

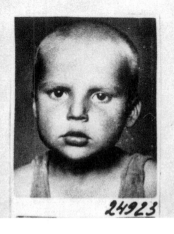
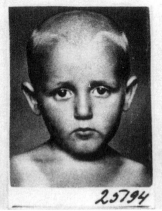
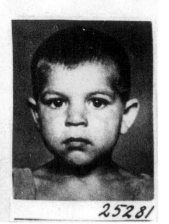

24673   24923   25794   25281

It would be wrong to say that the [prisoners'] children were kept on a starvation diet. They were given as much to eat as they could manage, and by my standards at the time the food seemed quite appetizing. For some reason, though, they all ate like little convicts: hastily, with no thought for anything else, carefully wiping their tin bowls with a piece of bread, or licking them clean. I was struck by the fact that their movements were unusually well coordinated for children of their age. But when I mentioned this to Anya she made a bitter gesture of dismissal.

"Don't you believe it! That's only at mealtime, that's their struggle for existence. But hardly anyone asks for the potty—they haven't been trained to it. Their general level of development...well, you'll see for yourself...."

It suddenly came to me that Anastas and Vera were the only ones in the entire group who knew the mysterious word "Mamma." Now that their mother had been sent elsewhere, they sometimes repeated the word with a sad, puzzled intonation, looking around uncomprehendingly. "Look," I said to Anastas, showing him the little house I had drawn, "what's this?"

"Hut," the little boy replied quite distinctly.

With a few pencil strokes I put a cat alongside the house. But no one recognized it, not even Anastas. They had never seen this rare animal. Then I drew a traditional rustic fence around the house....

"Compound!" Vera cried out delightedly, clapping her hands with glee.

—*Eugenia Ginzburg:*
Within the Whirlwind

short years of the NEP. A terrifying life befell these children. Many spent time in camps and prisons, were forced to work under unendurable conditions, and undergo terrible degradations: Many young girls were raped by camp guards or criminals; many suicides years later were, in fact, echoes of these tragedies.

There were even special camps for relatives of the repressed, such as "Algiers" (the Akmolinsky Camp for Wives of Traitors of the

Motherland). But there were many wives in other camps as well; no special privileges were given for women. Nor were exceptions made

TOP: *Boris Efanov, "Stalin and Molotov, with their Children," 1947.*

OPPOSITE, BOTTOM: *Stalin greeting children at the XVIIIth Congress of the Communist Party, Moscow, 1939.*

My enthusiasm for my exalted post distinctly waned when I saw the kindergarten curriculum on which we had to base our educational activities....In the section "Training in Patriotism," the teacher was required to cultivate not only the feeling of love for the Soviet homeland but also the feeling of *hatred* for its enemies.

In the section on speech training, one had to study the poem "I'm a little girl, I sing and I play/I haven't seen Stalin but I love him each day."

At the music periods taught personally by the head, Claudia Vasilevna, the children had to learn by heart, in additon to the "Two Eagles" song [about Lenin and Stalin]..., various other songs on the same inexhaustible theme: "If Stalin were to visit us..." And then there was the song of the young sailors: "Dear Comrade Stalin, the days will soon go by..."

Attendance at the Preschool Methodology Center was obligatory. At the very first seminar I listened to a very solid report on methodology by Aleksandra Mikhailovna Shilnikova. She gave an assessment of a May Day matinee concert at one of the kindergartens and quoted the children's reactions on this festive occasion:

"We love Comade Stalin more than Mommy or Daddy," the children were supposed to have said. Then they had shouted in chorus:

"May Comrade Stalin live to be a hundred! No, two hundred! No, three hundred!"

And one of the little boys, Vladimir, was so proficient in politics that he had cried out:

"May Comrade Stalin live forever!"
—*Eugenia Ginzburg:*
Within the Whirlwind

ABOVE: *Mamlakat Nakhangova in the Kremlin, 1935. An entire mythology developed around this Uzbek girl, who was said to have learned to gather cotton with both hands at the same time, by tying her bag around her neck, thus increasing the kolkhoz cotton yield.*

LEFT: *Infants, apparently in a children's home, with a portrait of Stalin and Engelsina Chezkova, 1930s. The portrait of Stalin and Engelsina was another popular official icon. Children were often used to promote the image of a caring, paternal leadership.*

OPPOSITE, TOP: *Boys in children's home, 1930s, with portrait of Stalin and Engelsina in the background.*

OPPOSITE, BOTTOM: *Float of children, sports demonstration on Red Square, 1936, bearing a tondo portrait of Stalin and Engelsina.*

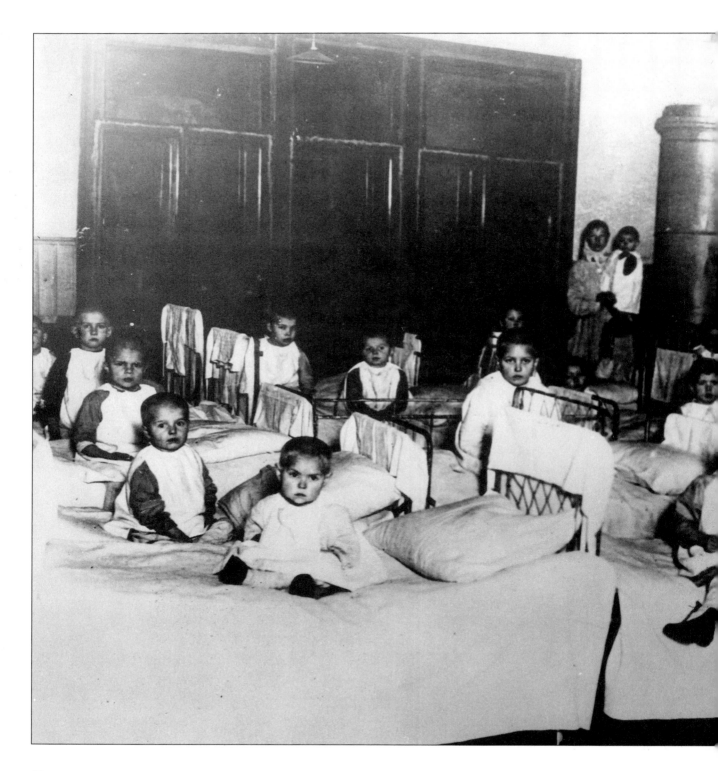

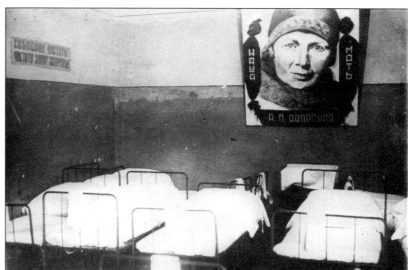

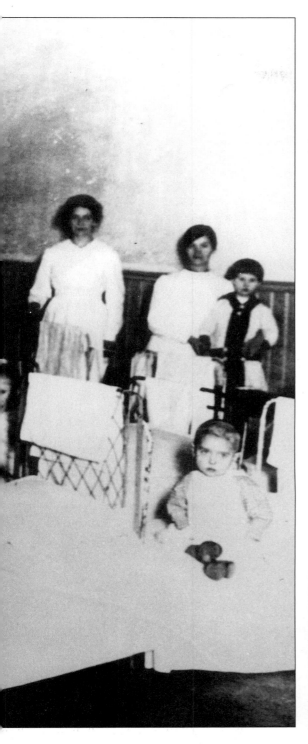

LEFT: *Girls' dormitory, orphanage, 1930s.*

ABOVE: *Orphanage dormitory, 1930s. The portrait reads, "Our Mother, A. P. Yavorskaya." Yavorskaya was a leader of the movement to "reform" homeless children after the civil war. The sign on the left wall says, "Observe cleanliness! Cleanliness is the guarantee of health."*

BELOW: *Orphanage children working in a shoe workshop, Minsk, 1923. Given the Yiddish banner on the wall, this may have been a home for Jewish children, which would not have been possible by the 1930s.*

for pregnant women or nursing mothers. Infants born in the camps, or nursing babies, were picked up with their arrested mothers and lived beyond the barbed wire in "children's complexes" or in special children's barracks.

The children of "repressed" people often ended up in children's homes or orphanages. The well-known Russian writer Vasily Aksyonov, who now lives in the United States, was interned in such a home. He wasn't quite five years old at the time his mother, the writer Eugenia Ginzburg, was arrested. His father was arrested soon after her. On his fifth birth-

---

BOTTOM: ***Poster saying, "We Will Raise a Generation Selflessly Devoted to Communism!"***
OPPOSITE, TOP: ***Boys lining up at the orphanage baths, 1930s.***
OPPOSITE, BOTTOM: ***Children weeding the vegetable garden of an orphanage, Moscow (the former Catherine Institute), 1920s.***

Mothers prepared their children for life by teaching them the sacred language of their seniors. "My children love Stalin most of all, and me only second," Pasternak's wife, Zinaida Nikolayevna, used to say. Others did not go so far, but nobody confided their doubts to their children: why condemn them to death? And then suppose the child talked in school and brought disaster to the whole family? And why tell it things it didn't need to know? Better it should live like everybody else....So the children grew, swelling the ranks of the hypnotized. "The Russian people is sick," Polia X. once said to me, "it needs to be treated." The sickness has become particularly obvious now that the crisis has passed and we can see the first signs of recovery. It used to be people with doubts who were considered ill.
—*Nadezhda Mandelstam:*
Hope Against Hope

day the "Leader, Father, and best friend of children" sent a representative of the NKVD to fetch him. He was taken to a special reception center for children of Enemies of the People. It was only after a long search that his father's brother, who had miraculously remained free, was able to find the child, get him released into his custody, and bring him back into the world.

When parents were arrested as "Enemies of the People," children were encouraged to renounce them. Julia Piatnitskaya, wife of the arrested Bolshevik Osip Piatnitsky, recorded the words her son wrote in his diary: "It's too bad that they didn't shoot

ВОСПИТАЕМ ПОКОЛЕНИЕ, БЕЗЗАВЕТНО ПРЕДАННОЕ ДЕЛУ КОММУНИЗМА!

Papa, seeing as he's an enemy of the people." Children were in fact systematically taught to denounce their parents: The Pioneer Scout Pavlik Morozov, around whom an entire cult grew up, had denounced his father to the NKVD for being connected to the kulaks. After Pavlik's death, supposedly at the hands of enraged kulaks, he was glorified as a national hero. In recent years, the writer Yuri Druzhnikov has studied the history of the Pavlik Morozov legend and noted certain curious facts: Pavlik was not in fact a Pioneer Scout; he was goaded into denouncing his father by his jealous mother, whom his father had left. Questions have also been raised about who actually killed Pavlik, and it has been suggested by some that it was agents of the NKVD who needed a *cause célèbre* for public consumption. They were successful: The legend of the Young Pioneer hero has not yet entirely died out. Many of the monuments erected in his honor still stand, and streets are still named after him. Only very recently, after the failed coup in August 1991, have some statues of Pavlik been dismantled.

By a decree issued April 7, 1935, children were brought under the same criminal statutes as adults: The age limit for the death penalty was lowered to twelve years of age. Alexander Orlov, a high-placed NKVD functionary who defected to the West in the late 1930s, wrote that Ezhov (who was Commissar of Internal Affairs at the time, though he, too, was soon removed and shot) "gave orders for

---

ABOVE: ***Contingent of Young Pioneers, parade on Red Square, 1930s.***
OPPOSITE: ***Exercise class in the yard of an orphanage, Minsk, 1923.***

NKVD agents to be placed in every prison cell, disguised as arrestees. These agents were supposed to tell the other prisoners stories of ten- and twelve-year-old children taken out for execution together with their parents." In this way Ezhov hoped to break the will of those under investigation and force them to sign whatever statements the investigator wanted. But it was, in fact, true: Children were arrested and shot. Yuri Chirkov, a prisoner at Solovetsky Prison, arrested at age fifteen, wrote in his memoirs: "I remember that they didn't actually arrest me, but kidnapped me from home after I returned from school one day, and then took me to the Lubianka because of a denunciation, and my parents spent all night searching for their son in the Moscow morgues. I remember my first interrogation, which continued until three in the morning. All sorts of fantastic accusations were made: that I had tried to blow up bridges; that I had planned an assassination attempt against the Ukrainian Central Committee secretary, Kosior (who himself was shot three years later as an Enemy of the People); and even that I had organized an attempt on the life of Stalin himself."

The bitter irony of history is that even the children of the victors, the children of the executioners, were damaged for life, if not arrested themselves. The son of Genrikh Yagoda (Commissar of Internal Affairs, shot as an Enemy of the People) wrote to his grandmother (who had also been sent to a camp) before disappearing without a trace: "Dear Grandma,

Once again I didn't die, but it's not the time I already wrote you about. I am dying many times. Your grandson."

And Stalin's own children? They, too, were hostages of the system. Driven to despair by his father's indifference, Yakov Dzhugashvili, Stalin's son by his first marriage, tried to commit suicide. He botched the attempt, which only provoked his father's complete derision. Vasily and Svetlana grew up without a mother. Nadezhda Alliluyeva, Stalin's second wife, committed suicide in 1932. The reasons are not entirely clear, but Alliluyeva was brought up in a family of underground Bolsheviks, and she must have realized that Stalin was not leading the country in the direction that her father and brothers had fought for. Some people have suggested that Stalin himself shot his wife. However, the suicide version seems the more plausible. This is the opinion of one of Stalin's biographers, Dmitrii Volkonogov, who writes that Stalin experienced Alliluyeva's suicide as an act of betrayal. "He didn't seem to be at all aware that his roughness, and the lack of warmth and attention, had so cruelly wounded his wife that she decided on an extreme step in a moment of emotional disturbance and depression. Saying his farewells at the civil funeral held for Alliluyeva, Stalin didn't go to the cemetery."

Neither did Stalin love his son Vasily. In effect, General Vlasik raised the boy. He was sent to a regular school, where his identity was

The only link with a person in prison was the window through which one handed parcels and money to be forwarded to him by the authorities....

There was generally no conversation in the line. This was the chief prison in the Soviet Union, and the people who came here were a select, respectable and well-disciplined crowd....The only incident I saw was when two little girls in neatly starched dresses once came in. Their mother had been arrrested the previous night. They were let through out of turn and nobody asked what letter their name began with. All the women waiting there were no doubt moved by pity at the thought that their own children might soon be coming here in the same way. Somebody lifted up the elder of the two, because she was too small to reach the window, and she shouted through it: "Where's my mummy?" and "We won't go to the orphanage. We won't go home." They just managed to say that their father was in the Army before the window was slammed shut. This could have been the actual case, or it could have meant that he had been in the secret police. The children of Chekists were always taught to say that their father was "in the army"—this was to protect them from the curiosity of their schoolmates, who, the parents explained, might be less friendly otherwise. Before going abroad on duty, Chekists also made their children learn the new name under which they would be iiving there....The little girls in the starched dresses probably lived in a government building—they told the people waiting in line that other children had been taken away to orphanages, but that they wanted to go to their grandmother in the Ukraine. Before they could say any more, a soldier came out of a side door and led them away. The window opened again and everything returned to normal. As they were being led away, one woman called them "silly little girls," and another said: "We must send ours away before it's too late."

— *Nadezhda Mandelstam:*
Hope Against Hope

carefully concealed from his classmates. The teachers, of course, knew who he was. Liudmila Uvarova, one of his teachers, remembers the strict instructions she received from the principal of the school: "You may ask Comrade Stalin's son questions, you may even call him to the blackboard, but no criticisms—not a single one."

The boy grew spoiled in a situation where everything was permitted him, and everyone flattered him. Nothing had any value for him. Vasily became an Air Force pilot and served reasonably well, though the speed with which he was promoted clearly did not correspond to his actual accomplishments. By the end of the war he was a lieutenant general. But such advancement could not help this weak-willed and narcissistic man: He drank too much, and he married and divorced a number of times. Literally days after his father died, the thirty-two-year-old Vasily was dismissed from the Army for inappropriate behavior. No one had to bow and scrape before him any longer. He died young, in the late 1950s.

Being the daughter of the great Stalin did not bring happiness to Svetlana, either. In contrast to most of her peers, she had never known material deprivation. She was always well dressed and well groomed (in his memoirs, Khrushchev compares her to a fancy doll), and she was surrounded by servants ready to fulfill her every whim. Her father and all his associates called her the "Housekeeper" and pretended to follow all her "orders." Again, Khrushchev remarked on the superficiality of her well-being: "Her relations with her father were complicated. Her father loved her, but even his feelings of love were brutally expressed. It was the tenderness of a cat toward a mouse. This also weighed heavily on the child, later on the young girl, and finally on the young woman and mother."

Svetlana understood that her relatives, who at one time had visited frequently, were disappearing—her mother's brothers Fyodor and Pavel, her cousin Anna, the family of her older brother Yakov. Few of her mother's relatives would die of natural causes. Later, Stalin would destroy Svetlana's first love, the cinematographer Alexei Kapler. He was sent to the camps without trial. Stalin broke up her marriage to the engineer Moroz (Stalin disliked both of these men because they were Jews); under pressure from him she finally agreed to marry Zhdanov's son, whom she didn't love and whom she left soon after her father's death. In 1967 she astounded the world by asking for political asylum in the American embassy during a trip to India to bury her third husband, an Indian citizen.

Svetlana did not find happiness with her fourth husband in the United States. Not long after the beginning of perestroika, she attempted to return to the Soviet Union with her twelve-year-old American daughter. But she no longer felt at home either in Moscow or in Georgia. She left the Soviet Union once again and now lives in the West.

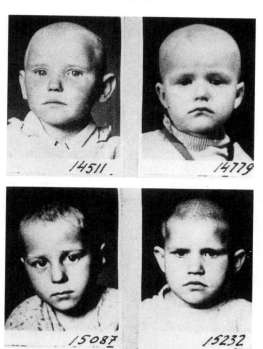

All Stalin's Men

The members of Stalin's Politburo and his other close associates inevitably kept him company in the screening room. All were imbued with the aura of legend for Ganshin. It was only after having worked in the Kremlin awhile, and having had the opportunity to see each of them and hear the stories of the guys in Stalin's guard, that Ganshin developed his own attitude toward each of them. Some he liked, some he was indifferent to, others he didn't care for at all.

If someone had told Ganshin that these "comrades" had more in common with gangsters than with faithful Communists, he would have been furious. But this was the view expressed by no less than Anastas Mikoyan, a member of Stalin's (and later Khrushchev's and Brezhnev's) Politburo. The contemporary writer Ales Adamovich writes that in the late 1950s Mikoyan's old Bolshevik friends asked him why the rehabilitation of political prisoners from the Stalin era was proceeding so slowly and inconsistently. Couldn't all the trials simply be declared illegal? Mikoyan replied, "No, they can't. If they were, it would be clear that the country was not being run by a legal government, but by a group of gangsters." He thought silently for a moment and added, "Which, in point of fact, we were."

No one in the ruling circle was allowed to retain a clean conscience: When Stalin signed execution lists, for example, he would send them around, and it was extremely dangerous not to support his decision. Marshal Zhukov told the story of an army officer who wrote an appeal to Stalin just before being executed. The officer proclaimed his innocence and said he remained faithful to the Party. According to Zhukov, "Stalin wrote boldly on one corner of the letter: 'He's just lying! Shoot him.'—Stalin. Then came the other signatures: 'I agree.'—Molotov. 'I agree. What a scoundrel! A dog's death for a dog.'—Beria. 'Fanatic.'—Voroshilov. 'Bastard.'—Kaganovich. But they all knew perfectly well that this man had been extremely devoted to the Party." Everyone in Stalin's entourage worked in one way or another to consolidate his power. But this by no means guaranteed them peace of mind or any assurance about the Master's feelings for them. Over the years, Stalin did away with many of his closest associates.

Nikita Khrushchev remembers once hearing Stalin mutter, as if talking to himself, "I'm

---

OPPOSITE: *May 1 parade on Red Square, Moscow, 1937. Note the portraits of Lenin, Stalin, and other members of the Politburo in the crowd.*

ABOVE: *Dimitrov, Khrushchev, Stalin, Voroshilov, Molotov, and Ezhov on the Lenin mausoleum tribune, November 1937.*

LEFT: *Budennyi, Stalin, Beria, Mikoyan, Kaganovich, Voroshilov, Molotov, Malenkov, and others reviewing the Air Force display at Tushino, 1939.*

OPPOSITE, TOP: *Stalin greeting the wives of Red Army officers, 1936. Most of these women's husbands were later shot.*

OPPOSITE, BOTTOM: *Boris Efanov, "Unforgettable Meeting," Stalin and the Politburo greeting the wives of heavy industry workers, 1937.*

done for. I don't trust anyone. Not even myself." Stalin trusted no one, and everyone was held hostage to his distrust. Even among his closest associates, there was almost no one who had not undergone the "test" of a close relative's arrest or execution. An attempt was made to arrest Voroshilov's wife (for once in his life he manifested a certain courage and resisted; strangely enough, this worked, and his wife was never imprisoned), and his daughter-in-law's parents were arrested. The husband of Shvernik's only daughter was executed—in fact, he was arrested while living in Shvernik's home; Poskrebyshev's wife, Bronislava Solomonovna, the mother of his two children, was accused of espionage and shot. Molotov's and Kalinin's wives were arrested, and Kaganovich's brother committed suicide rather than be arrested.

If Stalin acted in this manner with the wives and relatives of Politburo members, then one can imagine how he treated the families of people he considered political enemies. The wives of Bukharin, Shliapnikov, Sokolnikov, Bela Kun, Yakir, and many many others ended up in the camps. The wives of Tukhachevsky, Uborevich, and Gamarnik were shot. The frequency with which high Soviet functionaries committed suicide prior to their arrest, or at the moment of their arrest, can be partly explained by the desire to avoid torture, but also by the hope of saving their relatives. By 1938 there was no longer any doubt what fate awaited them.

BELOW: *Voroshilov and Stalin, 1937.*

OPPOSITE, ABOVE: *Voroshilov and Stalin Commemoration cups, from a tea service for sixteen, USSR Museum of the Revolution.*

OPPOSITE, BELOW: *Alexander Gerasimov, "Stalin and Voroshilov in the Kremlin," 1938. Stalin allowed a minor cult of personality to develop around Voroshilov, who was often portrayed in paintings and posters.*

Kliment Voroshilov was perhaps Ganshin's favorite Politburo member. He was a man of the people, a simple carpenter from Lugansk who had risen to the heights of the country's government. And, thought Ganshin, wasn't this one of the Revolution's great achievements, that so wonderful a talent, doomed under the czar, could now rise to a position of responsibility?

For almost fifteen years Voroshilov was head of the Red Army as the People's Commissar of Defense. His military feats during the Civil War were legend. Books were written about him, and songs were sung. Children learned by heart the poems of the Jewish poet Lev Kvitko: "I wrote a letter to Klim Voroshilov. Comrade Voroshilov, people's commissar!…" Expert marksmen in the Army were awarded a special badge distinguishing them as "Voroshilov sharpshooters." Alexander Gerasimov's painting *Stalin and Voroshilov in the Kremlin* was reproduced in millions of copies. The two great men walked side by side, friends and colleagues, against the background of the ancient Kremlin towers. Though Stalin was usually jealous of his associates, he never objected to Voroshilov's fame and popularity, the secondary cult of personality that grew up around him. He needed Voroshilov to play the role of popular hero, and he knew the value of such heroes.

The historian Yuri Geller, who has studied Voroshilov's activities during the Civil War period, has not discovered anything particularly worthy of praise. He was Commissar of Internal Affairs of the Ukraine at the time, and failed to quell the uprising of the Ataman Grigorev. Nor was Voroshilov able to retain Kharkov, which he surrendered to the White Army officer Denikin in 1919. Voroshilov was brought up before a military tribunal, which treated him patronizingly. Giving him his due for past service in the underground before the Revolution, the court noted that being a nice guy wasn't a profession; moreover it didn't make for a good military man.

It is now known that many of the Civil War victories attributed to Voroshilov during the

ABOVE: *Voroshilov and Stalin, 1920s.*

Stalin era were either accomplished by others or simply invented. The most important factor in Voroshilov's rise was his political service to Stalin rather than any military acumen. In 1929, for Stalin's fiftieth birthday, he published an article titled "Stalin and the Red Army," in which he managed to attribute great merit to events that were utter failures, or that had in fact had a damaging effect on the Army. By exalting and praising the Master, Voroshilov elevated himself as well. This article was central to the shameless rewriting of the history of the Civil War that had begun immediately in the wake of the war, as early as 1923.

Stalin valued the efforts of the People's Commissar. He had no illusions about Voroshilov's military talents, intellect, or human qualities. But that was not what he was needed for: Stalin needed people who would follow orders, especially given the purges that were about to begin.

"As a connoisseur of military affairs," Marshal Zhukov wrote in his memoirs, "Voroshilov was weak, of course, since other than participation in the Civil War he had no practical or theoretical base in the military arts, and therefore in his leadership of the Defense Commissariat, in the business of building up the armed forces and making military decisions, he had to rely on his closest assistants."

Voroshilov subsequently betrayed the assistants who had covered up his own incompetence: He was a key figure in the organization of mass repressions against the military leadership. Voroshilov's signature stands on lists of thousands of officers who were dismissed from the Army as a prelude to arrest. The losses among ranks of army officers were quite spectacular. The following list testifies to this: Of five marshals of the USSR, the Stalinist repressions removed three; of five top-level commanders, three were eliminated; all 10 second-level commanders were lost; of 57 corps commissars, 50 were lost; of 186 division commanders, 154; of 16 army commissars of the first or second level, all; of 456 colonels, 401. The Army was deprived of leadership and demoralized. Standards of battle-readiness and discipline thus fell, which had catastrophic repercussions in the attack on Finland in November of 1939. In the end, with extraordinary difficulty, the Soviet Union

finally managed to defeat the armed forces of a much smaller, weaker country, at the cost of enormous Soviet casualties. "Victory at that price was actually a moral defeat," Nikita Khrushchev admitted later.

The repressions had even more disastrous consequences later, during the Second World War. Voroshilov, who had been removed from his position as Commissar of Defense after the Finnish campaign, was again returned to a position of responsibility. He was appointed commanding officer of the northwestern region, which included the Baltic countries and Leningrad, and once again demonstrated his total incompetence. He couldn't bring himself to evacuate the main base of the Baltic fleet from Tallinn to Kronstadt without Stalin's sanction, and when circumstances finally forced him to do so, the Germans had already reached the port by land and opened battery fire on the naval convoys carrying base workers and families of navy personnel. Tens of thousands of people were drowned. Voro-

BELOW: *Molotov, Stalin, and Voroshilov sitting in the audience during the meeting with the wives of Red Army officers, Moscow, 1936.*

ABOVE: *Left to right: Molotov, Khrushchev, Stalin, Kosior, and Chubar on the tribune of the Lenin mausoleum during a sports parade, Moscow, 1935.*

LEFT: *Left to right: Beria, Stalin, Malenkov, and Kalinin heading for the mausoleum, Moscow, May 1, 1941.*

OPPOSITE, TOP LEFT: *Stalin, flanked by Kalinin and Molotov inside the Kremlin, Nov. 7, 1934. Note the two men whose faces have been scratched out on the negative.* OPPOSITE, TOP RIGHT: *Left to right: Khrushchev, Stalin, Malenkov, Beria, and Molotov, on their way to the sports parade on Red Square, 1945. Stalin awarded himself the title of Generalissimo, although prior to that he had not held any military rank; Beria, here in uniform, was made a Marshal of the Soviet Union in 1945.* OPPOSITE, BOTTOM: *Stalin with Beria, Mikoyan, and Malenkov, heading for Red Square, May 1, 1946.*

shilov's command career ended in complete failure when the Germans surrounded Leningrad. As a result the city was blockaded for nine hundred days and millions of people starved to death.

In other, analogous circumstances, officers were shot without hesitation or mercy. Stalin did not touch Voroshilov, however, or even subject him to public criticism: He was simply removed from his command position. Voroshilov also managed to survive after the war. He continued on as a member of Stalin's Politburo, and later, Khrushchev's. In 1957, he wisely abstained from the first, aborted attempt to remove Khrushchev and change the course of his reforms, which resulted in the political "deaths" (though not the executions, as would have been the case under Stalin) of Molotov, Malenkov, and Kaganovich. Voroshilov received a high-level, purely decorative position as President of the Presidium of the Supreme Soviet of the USSR. His duties included awarding government prizes and medals (previously called Stalin Prizes), and attending formal receptions. He, too, received a few medals, and the titles of Hero of the Soviet Union and Hero of Socialist Labor. When he died in 1969, the newspapers published a front-page obituary.

Molotov was Stalin's "shadow"—in photographs they often stood next to each other. His extraordinary capacity for work and his organizational abilities were well known. It was no accident that Stalin placed him in many different posts at moments of great importance: He worked as president of the Council of People's Commissars, and as Minister of Foreign Affairs; during the war he was a member of the State Defense Committee.

Molotov was often referred to as Stalin's club. During struggles with the political opposition, Stalin always promoted him whenever it was necessary to strike the first blow; Molotov was able to make that blow palpable. Among other things, Stalin valued Molotov because he never showed any ambition to supplant the Master.

The fact that Stalin appreciated Molotov is evident if only from the number of

cities, villages, collective farms, and factories named after him. (Under Khrushchev the practice of naming streets, cities, and organizations in honor of living people was discontinued. After the aborted coup of 1957, when Molotov and Kaganovich were in political disgrace, the city of Molotov went back to its old name of Perm, and the Moscow metro was renamed in honor of Lenin.) But another indication of the special position Molotov occupied among Stalin's associates (as Khrushchev would later say) was the fact that he was the only one Stalin permitted to have his own views. Stalin allowed Molotov to voice his opinion, even when the leader didn't like what he heard.

Stalin's attitude to his "shadow" was not without its limits, however. As mentioned ear-

lier, Molotov's wife was arrested and spent years in the camps; she was released after Stalin's death. Strangely, the experience of the labor camps did not affect Molotov's political convictions, nor those of his wife, Polina Zhemchuzhina. They remained convinced Communists, Stalinists, to the end of their lives. Though he was essentially removed from political life after the unsuccessful

ABOVE: *Molotov speaking at the celebration of the 22nd anniversary of the Revolution, 1939. Many of the figures sitting at the table in this photograph seem to have been retouched or cut out and replaced with others.*
OPPOSITE: *Stalin voting in the first Supreme Soviet elections, Moscow, 1937. In the background are Molotov and Voroshilov.*

OPPOSITE, TOP: *Left to right: Stalin, his second wife, Nadezhda, Voroshilov and his wife at the dacha, late 1920s/early 1930s. Unlike other Politburo members, Voroshilov resisted his wife's arrest, and thus she was one of the few Politburo wives who was not imprisoned.*

OPPOSITE, BOTTOM: *Molotov and his wife, Polina Zhemchuzhina, with Stalin and Nadezhda Alliluyeva, late 1920s.*

ABOVE: *Kalinin, Stalin, and Molotov examining an issue of Pravda, 1930. Both Molotov's and Kalinin's wives were arrested and sent to prison camps. Kalinin's wife was let out briefly to attend her husband's funeral; after Stalin's death, Molotov's wife was released and returned to her husband.*

RIGHT: *Poster of Politburo members, ca. 1946. Top, left to right: A. A. Andreev, K. E. Voroshilov, A. A. Zhdanov, L. M. Kaganovich, M. I. Kalinin. Bottom: A. I. Mikoyan, V. M. Molotov, N. S. Khrushchev, L. P. Beria, N. M. Shvernik.*

OPPOSITE, TOP: *Kirov, Kaganovich, Ordzhonikidze, Stalin, and Mikoyan inside the Kremlin walls, 1932.*

OPPOSITE, BOTTOM: *Stalin with Kirov's body, which lay in state in the Hall of Columns, Moscow, 1934. Kirov was murdered, presumably on Stalin's orders, in December 1934.*

ABOVE: *A. S. Yenukidze, Stalin, and Maxim Gorky sitting on the steps of the Lenin mausoleum, 1932. In the show trials of the late 1930s, both Yagoda and Yenukidze were accused of involvement in Gorky's death. If, indeed, the writer was poisoned, it is assumed that this could only have been on Stalin's orders.*

RIGHT: *Molotov, Stalin, and Ordzhonikidze carrying Gorky's bier, 1936.*

ABOVE: *Stalin and Ordzhonikidze, 1936.*
RIGHT: *Voroshilov, Molotov, Kaganovich, and Stalin carrying Ordzhonikidze's bier, 1937.*
OPPOSITE: *Presidium of the 31st anniversary of the Revolution celebrations, Moscow, 1948.*

attempt to overthrow Khrushchev in 1957 (he was named Soviet ambassador to Mongolia) and was excluded from the Party, Molotov was not executed. There can be little doubt, however, that had he himself been able to hold the upper hand in that affair, Khrushchev would have been shot. Molotov was famous for his stubbornness, and indeed, after twenty-seven years, during the short-lived rule of Chernenko, he managed to have himself reinstated in the Party. He was then ninety-four years old. He died in 1986, at age ninety-six, without having renounced his past. In interviews with him, published after his death, he continued to maintain that the repressions of the 1930s had been necessary and that the annexation of the Baltics, the western Ukraine and western Byelorussia were part of his primary task as Minister of Foreign Affairs—"to expand as much as possible the limits of our fatherland."

Kaganovich was disliked by Ganshin and the other members of the Kremlin guard (the only one they disliked more was Beria), because of his crude behavior. Once Kaganovich kicked a member of the guard who stood in his way. He kicked him so hard that the fellow had to be put in the hospital, and was lucky his spine hadn't been bro-

---

TOP: *Voroshilov, Molotov, Stalin, and Ezhov visiting the Moscow-Volga Canal, 1937. Note that the photograph has been extensively retouched or perhaps collaged. Ezhov was arrested in late 1938 and reportedly shot.*

ken. In his memoirs Khrushchev tells stories of Kaganovich's self-ingratiating personality: In front of Stalin, Molotov, and Voroshilov he would "run around like a toady on tiptoe and wag his tail." Ganshin himself was not anti-Semitic, and his dislike of Kaganovich had nothing to do with his being a Jew. The fact that Kaganovich was a Jew and a member of Stalin's Politburo only confirmed the ideals of fraternity and equality that had been drummed into Ganshin in school.

Kaganovich, too, underwent Stalin's "loyalty test." He had a brother, Mikhail, a member of the Bolshevik Party since 1905, who held the position of Minister of Aviation. Stalin told Kaganovich that it had been proved beyond a doubt that his brother was hobnobbing with the right wing, that Hitler had prepared a position for him in the future government. "He must be treated according to the law," was all Kaganovich could say, though he knew full well that the only law in the country was Stalin's will. Mikhail didn't wait to be arrested, but shot himself in 1938.

Stalin valued Kaganovich's incredible energy. "If we're talking about capacity for work," wrote Khrushchev, "he was a tempest. He worked as long as he had the strength, didn't spare himself at all, and didn't worry about the time." Stalin liked and appreciated his organizational abilities, and his absolute lack of a personal opinion in political questions. Without even looking into the details of an issue, he would declare, "I'm in complete agreement with Comrade Stalin." He was always ready to follow the leader's every command unquestioningly.

Kaganovich carried out brutal repressions during his tenure as Minister of Transportation. The railways, of course, did not work any better for this (all the best specialists were arrested), but the reports improved: Terror forced people to conceal problems for fear of punishment. Kaganovich never tired of reporting to the Master on his achievements in exposing class enemies: "In the political apparat of the commissariat of transportation we've exposed 220 people. 485 former gendarmes have been dismissed, 220 Social Revolutionaries and Mensheviks, 572 Trotskyites, 1415 White officers, 285 saboteurs, 443 spies. All of them were connected with the counter-revolutionary movement."

Kaganovich was the only member of Stalin's Politburo who lived to see the dismemberment of the totalitarian government established by Stalin. Kaganovich died in July 1991, at age ninety-eight. In his last years he lived in complete isolation, saw no one, and refused all requests for interviews. The press accused him of Stalinist crimes and invited him to visit the graves of people he had ordered executed. But he was not brought to trial. Nor, for that matter, were any of the people involved in the Stalinist repressions, with the exception of Beria.

Ganshin saw Mikhail Kalinin as a sympathetic figure, as did most people. A nice old man. Harmless. Ganshin liked his peasant origins, his wedge-shaped Russian beard, and his kind, slightly crafty countenance. Kalinin was the token representative of Russian peasantry on the Politburo, a "salt of the earth" figure useful for maintaining the fiction of a kind, caring government. Towns and cities were named after him, and there was a Kalinin Museum in Moscow until very recently. But, alas, Kalinin did nothing for the peasants he supposedly represented. He was a purely decorative figure whose main job was to award medals and prizes at official functions.

Last but hardly least among Stalin's men was Lavrenty Beria. Never in the entire history of Russia has the chief of the secret police been as all-powerful a figure as was Lavrenty Pavlovich Beria. In the Soviet period the secret police acquired far more extensive powers than they had had under the czars. Immediately after the October Revolution the Bolsheviks created the Extraordinary Commission (the Cheka). Chekists (agents of the Cheka) proudly called themselves the "guardian angels of the Revolution," "its shield and sword." The Cheka newspaper, *The Red Sword,* defined the organization's credo: "Everything is permitted us."

What the slogan "Everything is permitted us" meant in actuality is illustrated by descriptions of the Cheka cellars in cities won from the White Army. At times these cellars were seven inches deep in blood mixed with smashed skull and bone fragments, teeth, and pieces of scalp and skin. This was an organization that needed no permission to arrest even a prosecutor, or to execute anyone without trial.

Over the years, the organization changed its name (Cheka, GPU, OGPU, NKVD, KGB), and its chiefs (Dzerzhinsky, Menzhinsky, Yagoda, Ezhov, Beria, Serov, Shelepin, Semichastnyi, Andropov, Chebrikov, Kriuchkov). Some periods were more bloody than even the Civil War era, while others were, in the words of Nadezhda Mandelstam, "vegetarian times." But the organization's motto remained the same.

In December 1938 Lavrenty Beria became head of the NKVD. How did Beria come to such a high, powerful position? In the postwar years, some parts of the secret of his rise to power through the Caucasian GPU have come to light. And a few things are known about how Beria earned Stalin's approval. For instance, Beria gave Stalin

BELOW: *The young Beria, l927.*

ABOVE: ***Beria and members of the NKVD, 1930s.***

pride of place in his ghostwritten book on the history of the revolutionary struggle in the Caucasus. But during his "trial," other versions of his methods, no doubt many of them invented for dramatic effect, were made public. In one story, once Stalin visited his *dacha* in the Caucausus. He and Beria were driving along a twisting mountain road. Beria suddenly became alarmed and ordered the driver to stop. He leaped out of the car. There was a scuffling in the bushes, and a figure could be glimpsed. Beria pulled his gun and fired; the man in the bushes fell. They found a loaded gun on him. It looked as if he was planning to assassinate Stalin. Stalin didn't know that his savior, Beria, had himself staged the scene and planted the "assassin"— though, of course, without telling the man what his role was to be.

Since Beria's death, much has been written about him as a master of political provocation, a treacherous, insidious, and wily individual. But this isn't the only side to Beria. The Lubianka chief also knew how to make a good impression. Anna Larina, Bukharin's widow, saw a good deal of Beria in the early 1930s in Georgia. She writes convincingly that there didn't seem to be anything depraved about him. It was clear, Larina wrote, that he was smart, businesslike, and understood economics. He was hospitable, like all Georgians, appreciated the arts (his unique collection of classical records was well known), and loved sports. Larina noticed his soft, well-tended hands and sensual mouth. He was adventure-some and decisive in his judgments and actions. At that time, in the beginning of the 1930s, he resembled a Roman hero. Only a few years later his face would begin to acquire the features of a Roman patrician sated with the pleasures of the flesh.

Beria's organization had plenty of work throughout the fifteen years of his rule. Among the actions that cannot be overlooked was the execution of ten thousand Polish officers in the forest of Katyn (additional work was necessary to be able to present their deaths as the work of the Fascist occupiers). There was also the preventative deportation of hundreds of thousands of inhabitants of the Baltics, Bessarabia, the western Ukraine and Byelorussia, all of whom came under Stalin's rule thanks to the Molotov-Ribbentrop Pact. Also, the relocation of entire peoples Stalin didn't like to remote areas of the country: the Volga Germans, Crimean Tartars, Kalmyks, and others (these people were usually given twenty-four hours' notice of relocation, and as many as half of those relocated perished along the way).

During the war, Beria founded the organization called SMERSH (an acronym for "Death to Spies"). SMERSH's task was to expose untrustworthy people in the army. Many were shot. During the war, special divisions existed that stood behind the front-line soldiers, who knew that if they refused to attack and tried to retreat, even if advancing were utter folly, they would be met by a bullet from the rear.

After the war, Beria and his men were busy with the show trials in the occupied countries of Eastern Europe. There were also the "displaced persons" and war prisoners to be dealt with. Stalin considered all of them traitors: They were sent straight from German concentration camps to Soviet ones. The Cossacks, who had been subjected to near genocide even in Lenin's time, came in for particularly harsh treatment.

When Ganshin went to the theater, he informed the Special Section where he was going and in what seat number he would be sitting. He could get tickets to any theater through the Kremlin; the seats were always excellent, and close to the aisle, so that if he were called he could leave quickly. That was the case one night in September 1947, when he and his wife went to the Bolshoi Theater to see *Swan Lake*. Ganshin knew that Stalin loved this ballet, so he had been looking forward to it for some time. And truly, the great Soviet ballerina Ulanova danced divinely! But in the middle of the third act, a quiet voice suddenly asked him to come to the exit. A car was waiting for him on the street. The driver sped off, and a minute later they entered the Kremlin gates. A sealed film canister already stood in the projectionist's booth; the accompanying NKVD officer, a major, would not allow him to break the seal until the viewer had arrived in the room. Ganshin immediately recognized the bald skull and rolls of fat at the neck.

Ganshin was invited into the screening room. Without turning around, Beria said, "You know what happens to anyone who tells state secrets?" "I know, Lavrenty Pavlovich," said Ganshin. "Off with his head is what happens," said Beria, though Ganshin knew this all too well. "So don't forget. Go on and show the film."

Ganshin returned to the projectionist's booth and opened the canister in the presence of the

OPPOSITE: *Kalinin, Beria, and Molotov, 1930s.*

major. He loaded the projector. On the screen there appeared the slowly expanding mushroom of an enormous explosion. Then a forest blown away by a fire storm, buildings falling like card houses, burning animals—frightening pictures of nuclear destruction. So it's not only the Americans who have a bomb, thought Ganshin; we have one, too. He realized that Beria had directed the work of its creation.

It wasn't an easy project. Yes, the Soviet Union had outstanding nuclear physicists, but they couldn't possibly have managed to make a bomb by 1947 if Beria's agency hadn't provided them with scientific information stolen from the West. Neither would it have been possible without the forced labor of engineers and scientists interned in *sharashkas*, like the one Solzhenitsyn describes in his novel *The First Circle*. It wouldn't have been possible without the slave labor of prisoners to build the necessary factories for the bomb's manufacture. Stalin appreciated Beria's work for the government: He awarded him the title of

Marshal of the Soviet Union, and he soon made him a member of the Politburo.

Beria knew how to take care of himself as well. A government airplane regularly brought him fresh vegetables from Georgia, a special Georgian cheese called *sulguni*, and fresh, young wine. In Moscow Beria's sexual appetites were legend among the high echelons. Many famous beauties—actresses and singers among them—were honored with his attentions, after which their careers took a sharp turn upward. The few who failed to reciprocate his attentions met a harsher fate. Zoya Fyodorova, a famous movie actress of the 1930s and 1940s, was invited to Beria's house for dinner. "Come over here, my little monkey," he said to her, indicating that she should sit on his lap. "You're an old gorilla yourself," the actress answered. She was in love with the American naval attaché, and had no intention of betraying him. "You're camp dust," Beria said to her. She spent twelve years in the camps, where Viktoria, the daughter of

the American attaché was born. The accusation was standard: espionage.

Often it was possible to see two black limousines driving slowly down the streets of Moscow, hugging the sidewalks so that the occupants could see the women walking by. Behind the thick glass of the first car, a pince-nez could be made out, which Muscovites readily recognized from Beria's portraits.

That's what happened one evening when the second limousine stopped near a fifteen-year-old schoolgirl. A nice-looking officer of the NKVD invited her to get into the car. It was impossible to refuse: Everyone knew quite well what the NKVD was. The girl was taken to a private house on the Moscow Ring Road.

When she returned home, she refused to tell her parents what had happened. The girl went mad and committed suicide. The doctor who examined the body established that she had been raped.

Stalin was far from absolutely certain of the loyalty of his chief of secret police. Beria was not like the others who had held the position. Yagoda and Ezhov

ABOVE: *Beria and Stalin on the Black Sea, 1930s.*
OPPOSITE: *Beria with Svetlana at the **dacha**, 1935. Stalin is sitting in the background.*

were simply functionaries; Beria, however, was a partner, an equal capable of proposing approaches that Stalin was ready to accept; their political methods were identical. But he wasn't about to trust him with everything; Beria had too much power and influence.

The "comrades" in the Politburo became increasingly wary of Beria: He was becoming more and more influential. Everyone played up to him. They conferred with him beforehand on issues they wanted to present to Stalin; nothing got decided without Beria's support. It was becoming obvious to everyone that he was the top candidate as Stalin's successor. Beria himself, it seems, had no doubt about it.

He was mistaken. After Stalin's death, Khrushchev was able to unify Molotov, Mikoyan,

Once he was First Secretary in Georgia, it didn't take Beria long to reach Moscow, where he began his long reign in 1938. From then on he saw my father every day. His influence on my father grew and grew and never ceased until the day of my father's death.

I speak advisedly of his influence on my father and not the other way around. Beria was more treacherous, more practiced in perfidy and cunning, more insolent and single-minded than my father. In a word, he was a stronger character. My father had his weaker sides. He was capable of self-doubt. He was cruder and more direct than Beria, and not so suspicious. He was simpler and could be led up the garden path by someone with Beria's craftiness. Beria was aware of my father's weaknesses. He knew the hurt pride and the inner loneliness. He was aware that my father's spirit was, in a sense, broken. And so he poured oil on the flames and fanned them as only he knew how. He flattered my father with a shamelessness that was nothing if not Oriental. He praised him and made up to him in a way that caused old friends, accustomed to looking on my father as an equal, to wince with embarrassment.

Beria's role was a terrible one for all our family. How my mother feared and hated him! And it was her friends—Alexander Svanidze, his wife Maria, his sister Mariko who was Yenukidze's secretary, to say nothing of Yenukidze himself—who were the first to fall, the moment Beria was able to convince my father that they were hostile to him.

—*Svetlana Alliluyeva:*
Twenty Letters to a Friend

Malenkov, and all the others around him, since they understood that no good would come of appointing Beria to the position of General Secretary. Beria was arrested at a meeting of the Politburo, by Marshal Zhukov.

The revelations that followed—even though much was not made public—produced a feeling of shock in the country when some of the information did come out. In previous years there had, of course, been plenty of sensational trials, but they always had a political coloring; this was not the case with Beria. Although he was called an agent of English imperialism, he was actually presented as a plain scoundrel, a sadist and pervert, a man devoid of all principles, scruples, or morals.

In Beria's private house there was said to be a tub of highly concentrated sulfuric acid; those people Beria wanted to do away with quietly, without arrest or trial, disappeared without a trace. There were other ways of getting rid of bothersome people. Someone would suddenly be sent on a business trip to Leningrad and would die in the train on the way (almost all had tickets in the same train compartment). Some were called to Ulianovsk, where in a special safe house they would be pricked with a poisoned needle concealed in a cane. No one really knows how many secret victims there were. But it is known that in the Ulianovsk apartment alone more than three hundred people were killed.

After his arrest, Beria was held in a cement bunker at the headquarters of the Air Force in Moscow. He was impudent and demanded that women be brought to him. He evinced no guilt, no feeling of responsibility for what he had done. It isn't hard to understand his atti-

---

I was in the kitchen—boiling a repulsively ugly crab under the direction of Aunt Zina, who was on duty that day—at the moment when our permanently plugged-in radio suddenly started regaling us with details from Lavrenty Beria's biography. On hearing that he was an agent of the Tsarist secret police, an English spy, and an arrant enemy of the people, Aunt Zina and I left the boiling crab to the mercies of fate and stared at each other in mute disbelief.

"Aunt Zina," I said, "Aunt Zina, would you please repeat what you just heard over the radio?"

"Why me? What do you think you heard?" she shouted, advancing on me almost aggressively.

"I didn't quite catch it.... Or perhaps I misheard it...."

"Well, I haven't been able to make sense of it all for a long time now. You're educated folk, you read newspapers and talk on the telephone....It's not for me to repeat things like that. We're simple folk, we didn't go to no university."

I quickly got ready and rushed off to see Anton at his new place of work.

"Did you hear?"

"Shh, shh," he replied, "let's say nothing for the moment. I'll finish off here and we'll look in at the post office and check...."

I immediately realized what he had in mind. At the post office, above the registered-correspondence section, hung a portrait of Lavrenty Beria: a very intellectual face; a pince-nez; regular, in fact rather fine, features; and a thoughtful look.

Quite out of breath, we ran into the spacious hall of the post office. Above the head of the young lady who was dealing with registered letters, a large, dark, square, empty space yawned provocatively, almost cynically. It was apparent that the paint on the wall around had faded over the years.

—*Eugenia Ginzburg:*
Within the Whirlwind

tude. It wasn't simply that he alone had the key to a whole series of important government secrets, lists of agents who would be important to his successors, whoever they might be. He also knew that the men who held him behind bars were essentially just like him, or at least they bore almost as much responsibility for the regime's crimes. They all deserved their own Nuremberg. Beria was eliminated not for his crimes but because he was too dangerous for the others, because he had gone further in the pursuit of personal power than anyone else.

Beria was condemned to be shot. One of the officers guarding him, a colonel of the military secret service, asked for permission to carry out the sentence himself. He was the father of the fifteen-year-old schoolgirl who had gone

ABOVE: *Molotov, Stalin, Beria, and Malenkov on the Lenin mausoleum tribune, May 1, 1949.*

mad and committed suicide after having been raped by Beria. However, his request was not granted. Beria's execution was not an affair of personal vengeance. It was the very first reckoning with the Stalinist regime, although at the time few understood the direct link between the two.

After Beria was shot, a doctor was called in to examine the body. "There's nothing to examine!" he said. "I know him, he's been rotting for a long time. He's had syphilis since at least 1943."

Beria's trial forced society, perhaps for the first time, to think about itself. "Everything that I found out about him during the trial," the director Alexander Dovzhenko wrote in his diary, "was so revolting and disgusting, so criminal and pathologically vile, that it seemed it couldn't get any worse.... Who are we? What are we? Why was this possible?"

The War and Its Aftermath

Ganshin still remembers the night of the start of the war. He'd been at Stalin's *dacha* to show him a film, and he stayed over after a late screening. Yakov Dzhugashvili woke him up in the middle of the night. Everyone gathered in the kitchen. Yakov poured them all a drink. "Well, it's begun," he said.

War had been expected for a long time. Although relations with Germany had seemed good since the friendship pact had been signed in 1938, and a joint parade of Soviet and German troops had even been held in Brest on the occasion of the end of the Polish campaign in 1939, no one trusted the Germans. Ganshin preferred to keep his own council on the subject. You could be thrown in jail for "anti-German sentiment." Molotov had explained in his report at the time of the pact that the Soviet-German rapprochement was an alliance of principle, reflecting a profound similarity of position. Lev Mekhlis, the head of the Red Army political directorate, announced that if the imperialists started the Second World War, the Soviet Army would fight on enemy territory and increase the number of Soviet republics.

The number of republics had been on the rise. Latvia, Lithuania, and Estonia had expressed their desire to join the USSR (that's what they wrote in the papers; no one knew anything about any secret points in the Molotov-Ribbentrop Pact; even today, Ganshin still thinks such talk is all a bunch of lies); Bessarabia was brought in, and the Moldavian Republic was formed; after the war with Finland, the Karelo-Finnish region was established. The war with Finland hadn't been all that successful—many people had perished, although they didn't write about this in papers.

Stalin was publicly silent the first two weeks of the war. It was Molotov who addressed the people when the Fascists attacked on June 22, 1941. No one could understand why Stalin didn't speak out. The people couldn't imagine that their Master was frightened and depressed by the "betrayal" of Hitler, on whom he had placed such high hopes. Beria's version (which Khrushchev revealed many years later) would have seemed even more fantastic: that Stalin had wanted to resign, and when the Politburo members arrived at the *dacha* to convince him not to give up leadership of the country, he was confused and scared—afraid

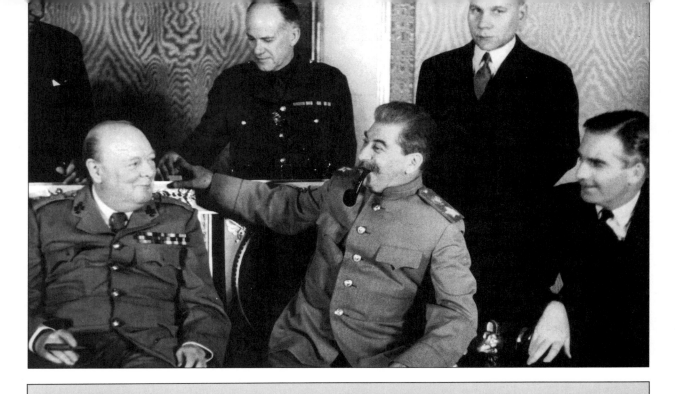

In August of 1942 Winston Churchill came to Moscow. One day Alexandra Nakashidze telephoned and told me I was to come into town. Churchill was having dinner in our apartment that night and my father had given orders that I was to be home. I went in wondering whether it would be all right to say a few words of English or better simply to remain quiet.

Our apartment was empty and depressing. My father's library was in Kuibyshev, and the bookshelves in the dining room were empty. Someone had telephoned from the Ministry of Foreign Affairs to explain the etiquette for dealing with foreigners, and the servants were fussing anxiously around.

Finally they all came down the corridor and went into the dining room. I followed. My father was in an unusually cordial frame of mind. He was in one of those amiable and hospitable moods when he could charm anybody. Patting me on the head, he said, "This is my daughter," and added, "She's a redhead!"

Churchill smiled and remarked that he had been red-haired, too, when he was a young man, but now look—and he waved a cigar in the direction of his head. He said that his daughter was in the Royal Air Force. I understood what he was saying but was too shy to say anything myself.

That's all that was said about me. The conversation went back to the usual guns, howitzers and airplanes. I understood nearly everything, including the fact that the interpreter, V. N. Pavlov, was giving an accurate translation. But I wasn't allowed to listen long. My father kissed me and told me to go on about my own business. I couldn't understand why he had wanted to show me off to Churchill. But I think I see why now. He wanted to seem at least a little like an ordinary human being. You could see he liked Churchill.

—*Svetlana Alliluyeva:*
Twenty Letters to a Friend

everyone wanted to run somewhere, anywhere. Vlasik was urgently sent to Kuibyshev to prepare for evacuating the government. The entire government, it was said, would be sent there.

Fortunately, Moscow was saved. The Germans were beaten back on the outskirts of the capital. This was the first significant Soviet victory of the war.

that they'd come to arrest him for doing nothing at such a fateful moment in the country's history. However, soon everything fell in place. Finally, on July 3, Stalin spoke on the radio and said: "Right is on our side. The enemy will be destroyed." Everyone breathed a sigh of relief. If Stalin had said it, then that's they way it would be.

There would be difficult moments, of course. Ganshin remembers the October 1941 panic in Moscow, when it seemed that the capital would be surrendered to the Germans. There was a rush to evacuate offices and factories. Some say that stores were abandoned, their doors left open. There was a huge crush at the stations, everybody was frantic to get on a train out of town. The huge expanse of Komsomol Square was packed with people;

OPPOSITE: *Churchill, Gusev, Stalin, Shchen, and Kerr Clark, at a reception in the Kremlin in 1944.*
ABOVE: *Churchill, Roosevelt, and Stalin at the Yalta Conference, 1945.*

Today it's hard for Ganshin to separate what happened in real life from what he saw on the movie screen. The movies seem even more real than life. In the movies there was no mention of the millions of Soviet prisoners who ended up in the trenches near Minsk, Kiev, Sevastopol. In the movies they didn't say anything about the best commanders being destroyed by Stalin and Beria before the war and even during it (but, indeed, the execution machine continued to work unabated through the war). And, of course, in the movies they wouldn't have dared even hint at what no one knew at the time: that Stalin had sought contact with Hitler to propose territorial concessions in exchange for cessation of hostilities.

In such films as *The Battle of Stalingrad, The Third Blow, The Fall of Berlin,* and *Oath,* a magnificent, wise, calm Stalin appeared on the screen. He always knew where the fatal blow could be struck at the Fascists, and always knew what the next blow would be. It was he who had said, "Victory will be ours." That's what he said, and that's what happened.

After I had left President Kalinin's office and gone to the Premier's apartment—and within a very few minutes after sitting down at the desk—I was perfectly amazed and almost struck dumb with surprise to see the far-end door of the room open and Stalin come in alone. I had not the remotest idea it was going to happen. In the first place, he is not the head of the state, and it is his purpose and theirs, apparently, to keep him apart from the state, and, as you know, no diplomat ever sees him officially or otherwise in a personal way. In fact, he avoids any such meeting. So closely had he been shielded from the public that it has almost become a historical event when he receives any foreigner.

Well, when he came in, of course, I stood up and approached him. He greeted me cordially with a smile and with great simplicity, but also with a real dignity. He gives the impression of a strong mind which is composed and wise. His brown eye is exceedingly kind and gentle.

A child would like to sit in his lap and a dog would sidle up to him. It is difficult to associate his personality and this impression of kindness and gentle simplicity with what has occurred here in connection with these purges and shootings of the Red Army generals, and so forth....

We sat down at the table and with an interpreter talked for two hours....It was really an intellectual feast, which we all seemed to enjoy. Throughout it we joked and laughed at times. He has a sly humor. He has a very great mentality. It is sharp, shrewd, and, above all things else, wise, at least so it would appear to me. If you can picture a personality that is exactly opposite to what the most rabid anti-Stalinist anywhere could conceive, then you might picture this man. The conditions that I know to exist here and his personality are just as far apart as the poles....

—*Joseph E. Davies:*
Mission to Moscow

T he war was over. Life had gotten a little easier. The ration card system was abolished at the end of 1947. There was a money reform, after which Ganshin's meager savings were reduced to nothing. But he wasn't upset. He had always earned his money honestly—so he'd earn some more. Ganshin's living quarters still weren't very good. Before the war he'd lived in a communal apartment, then he and his family had

moved to a Kremlin dormitory. The conditions there were a bit better, but not much—they had one room, opening onto a common hall, a common kitchen, and a toilet in the courtyard. At the beginning of the 1950s he was given a room in a real apartment on what is now Kutuzovsky Prospect. This was along the route that Stalin took from his *dacha* to the Kremlin, and so reliable people had been assigned housing there. It was a bit crowded with three people in one room (his daughter was thirteen now), but Ganshin had never lived any better, and most of the people he knew were worse off. Besides Ganshin there was only one neighbor in the apartment, an officer of the guard who also worked in the Kremlin.

OPPOSITE: *Joseph Davies, Stalin, and Molotov at a reception in the Kremlin, 1943.*
ABOVE: *Stalin, Malenkov, Beria, and others with Zhou En-Lai at the signing of the Sino-Soviet Pact in the Kremlin in 1952.*

Everything seemed to be improving, prices were lowered every year, and the country appeared to be recovering from the trauma of war. But still, there was disturbing news. Relations with the former Allies had deteriorated. They weren't grateful that Russia had saved them from Hitler. The war in Korea began. Ganshin knew that Russians were fighting in the North against the Americans. It wasn't wise to talk about this, but it wasn't really a secret, either.

The newspapers published alarming articles. One ideological campaign followed another. Either someone was trying to provoke a new world war, or there were trials of traitors in the new Socialist bloc countries. Serious failings were appearing in cultural politics. "Bourgeois remnants" were uncovered in music, film, literature, and biology. In all spheres of society the struggle with "cosmopolitanism" was on: People were encouraged to struggle against those who bowed and scraped before the West, who had forgotten that the great Russian people was responsible for all the most outstanding discoveries in science, technology, culture, and the arts.

"Cosmopolitan" was generally a code word for "Jews," but Jews were not the only ones included in these campaigns. The virus of anti-Semitism seems to have lain dormant in Stalin for some time, but it manifested itself abundantly during and after the war. (It is probable that the Jewish origins of many of his political associates-turned-"enemies" played some role: Trotsky, Zinovyev, Kamenev, Yagoda, Radek, Piatnitsky, and others.) Anti-Semitism, always the shame of Russia, was once again dragged out as a government affair, although in a somewhat different form than under the czars. If before the Revolution the limitations placed on Jews under the law were openly known to everyone, under Stalin they were shrouded in silence, though their existence was well known. A similar practice continued into the more liberal but equally hypocritical post-Stalin era. Government propaganda never tired of heralding the great fraternity of all Soviet peoples, a fraternity supposedly possible only under socialism. But the bloody national outbursts of recent, perestroika years have shown the price that was paid for this "fraternity."

The Jews' place was particularly unenviable: They were not accepted into institutes and universities, they were not given jobs or allowed to rise high in their careers. Entire areas of government, Party, and scientific work were inaccessible to Jews. A wave of repressions against Jewish culture began in the late 1940s and early 1950s. The Jewish Theater and Jewish publishing house were closed and many of the actors and editorial workers were imprisoned or shot. The entire Jewish Anti-Fascist Committee, which had done so much during the war to raise money for Russia from Jews all over the world, was arrested and shot.

The poets Lev Kvitko and Perets Markish were murdered; in 1948, the extraordinary actor Solomon Mikhoels was killed, his murder staged as a car accident.

The peak of Stalinist anti-Semitism, however, came at the end of 1952 and the beginning of 1953, when the notorious "Doctors' Affair" began. The newspapers informed the public that the MGB (KGB) had neutralized a large group of Kremlin Hospital employees who had disguised their criminal goal—to do away with Stalin—under the guise of charity and humanism. They had already managed to eliminate two of his most outstanding colleagues, it was said: Andrei Zhdanov and Alexander Shcherbakov. Most of the doctors were Jews. The anti-Jewish campaign snowballed.

Meetings were organized in workplaces all over the country to denounce "the murderers in white coats." Jews in all professions were fired from their jobs. Pogroms against the Jews had been officially "scripted," as had their "defense": The entire action was to be presented as an act of Stalin's great humanism. Despite the Jewish people's horrible crimes, Stalin was to manifest charity toward the Jews. A special issue of the newspaper *Pravda* was prepared with an article titled "The Russian People Save the Jewish People." Plans were made for a mass deportation of Jews to remote regions of Siberia. There are reports that transportation convoys had been organized and barracks prepared. As in all the earlier cases of deportations of the Germans, Kalmyks, Crimean Tatars, etc., a huge number of those deported were supposed to die along the way, this time from the "people's just anger."

The writer Abdulakhman Avtorkhanov, in his book *The Death of Stalin*, argues that the destruction of the Jews was not Stalin's goal per se, but that he was only planning to use this campaign to eliminate his closest associates—Beria, Molotov, Malenkov, and Kaganovich—who had become too powerful and presented a threat to his personal dictatorship. The doctors arrested were their personal physicians. The plots were not against their patients, Tass reported, but against the departed Zhdanov and Shcherbakov.

However, Stalin forgot that the colleagues he intended to eliminate this time around were graduates of his own school of politics. They themselves had arranged such scenarios with him in the past, and understood quite well what the absence of their names on the doctors' future victims list meant. They had to act without delay. Avtorkhanov argues that Beria convinced them of this and took the job of liquidating Stalin himself. He had been laying the groundwork for some time by getting rid of Vlasik and Poskrebyshev, and all those in Stalin's personal guard who were particularly devoted to him.

When Stalin fell ill, before any doctors were brought in (the *dacha* staff knew all his personal physicians well), a woman in a white coat is reported to have arrived at the *dacha* and given him an injection. Who was this woman? What sort of injection did she give the Master? Vasily Stalin had no doubt about who had sent her and for what purpose. "They killed him!" he shouted over the body of his dead father.

This is only a hypothesis, of course. It is impossible to prove or disprove. The last person who could have thrown some light on it, Lazar Kaganovich, took the secret with him to his grave. But still, this scenario deserves some attention. The Indian ambassador, U. K. Krishna Menon, who met Stalin two weeks before his death, did not observe any signs of worsening health in him. According to a doctor who claimed to have attended Stalin in his last years (his words were recorded by the former editor of *Izvestia,* I. Gronsky, who returned from the camps in 1955), the Master had no health complaints. His only problem was that he had trouble sleeping: "Stalin would suddenly awake and jump out of bed, shouting wildly; nightmares haunted him."

And one day we really did hear something that astounded not merely the whole world but even the old Kolyma hands. It was at the beginning of April.

"Listen!" shrieked Claudia Gusyev, flying into the kitchen. "Listen to the radio!"

The radio in the kitchen was kept permanently on, but it was always drowned out by the sputtering of gas primuses and kerosene burners and by the sound of women's voices. But this time there was instantaneous and complete silence. In the sudden silence we listened to the reading of the official announcement on the termination of the Doctors' Case—"the assassins in white gowns." The text obviously gave the announcer a lot of bother. His voice, so used to reciting triumphal achievements and heroic moments, sounded odd. His had been the voice of the Infallible State. But now, for the first time in the memory of the listeners, it was having to speak of its own errors. And not only of errors, but also of "illegal methods of investigation"! True, these strange words were pronounced somewhat indistinctly, as if they had to be forced out through the teeth, and with obvious effort. None the less, they were uttered. To our way of thinking this was the beginning of a new era.

"Illegal methods of investigation." Just think of it! They had come out with it at last. These four words became a vaccine injected under the skin of millions of Kolyma deportees and prisoners and produced irrepressible excitement—in all of them together and in each one of them individually....

—*Eugenia Ginzburg:*
Within the Whirlwind

Stalin's Funeral

Stalin's death was officially announced on March 5, 1953. Bulletins on his condition began to be published a few days earlier; it is possible that the official date of his death is incorrect and that the bulletins were issued to prepare the country, when in fact the Leader had already died.

The entire country mourned his death. Ganshin was especially affected. He had known him as a god and as a man. A god is supposed to be immortal. The embalmed body of Stalin-the-God would be placed in the Red Square mausoleum next to the body of Lenin-the-God, and together they would lie there for eternity.

It was hard for people to get used to the idea that their god had died. There was confusion and bewilderment. Those who had sincerely believed in Stalin couldn't conceive how they were going to live without him. Who would defend the country? Who would feed the people? Less naive people feared the ensuing struggle for the empty throne. They feared a new wave of repressions, or a civil war.

Stalin's body lay in state in the Hall of Columns at the Union House, not far from the Kremlin. The crowds of people wanting to say farewell to him were so large that the police couldn't control them. In various parts of the city center, the crowds panicked, and it is estimated that hundreds of people were crushed to death. Some even say the numbers ran in the thousands.

The embalmed body was placed in the Red Square mausoleum. At first it was planned that both Lenin and Stalin—along with the remains of the other Party activists buried in the Kremlin wall—would be moved to a Pantheon of Great People, as soon as such a structure could be built. But that idea was soon forgotten. Shortly after Khrushchev's attack on Stalinism at the XXIIth Party Congress, in October 1961, Stalin's body was removed from the mausoleum one night and reburied in the Kremlin wall. A granite bust was erected over his grave, which can be reached only by going through the mausoleum. Throughout the country, monuments and portraits of Stalin were taken down and destroyed, or put in storage. In intellectual circles this was greeted as a positive development: Stalin wasn't worthy of a place near Lenin. Some thirty years later, during perestroika, another point of view was to take hold of the country. Why should Lenin be mummi-

---

OPPOSITE: *Crowd lining up to view Stalin's body, Moscow, March, 1953.*

fied in a mausoleum, rather than be buried in the earth, as is the custom in European countries? Why should *he* be deified by a people to whom he brought so much affliction?

Under Soviet power, but particularly during the Stalin era, all traces of independent thought and action were systematically suppressed and punished. The methods and targets of suppression were various. In the relatively "vegetarian" times of the post-Revolution period, hundreds of the best representatives of the creative intelligentsia, including outstanding philosophers such as Berdiaev, Lossky, Frank, and Fedotov, were banished from the country. During Stalin's "cannibalistic" reign, similar goals were achieved with brutal physical methods: labor camps and executions. As a result, the country's infrastructure of creative, active people—of all classes—was nearly virtually destroyed.

In its place a class of "functionaries" arose. There were functionaries in all professions. The executioners themselves were functionaries. Under Stalin this profession was quietly integrated into society, and the numbers of accomplices and informers grew to unprecedented proportions. Today, under perestroika, these people continue to live out their lives in government *dachas*, on high government pensions. Not a single one of them has ever been tried for the crimes of the terror. Stalinism has not had its Nuremburg.

Despite the horrors of the past, the country is

ABOVE: *Panoramic view of crowd during Stalin's funeral.*

now awakening. Normal human relations and moral values are being reasserted. Religious faiths of all kinds are reviving. The common human desire to own something, to have a material basis for self-worth, is no longer punished. The word "business" is no longer a criminal accusation in Russia. Sartre's existential formula "What's important is not what has been done to us, but what we ourselves have done with what has been done to us" applies to the contemporary Russian situation more than ever.

As for Ganshin, after Stalin's death he continued to work in the Kremlin for two years, not as a projectionist, but as a member of the Kremlin Guard. He preferred to show films, but he had to think about his pension, to work enough years to receive a bonus for time served. He did so, and then returned to the movies—first working in the Cinema-Photographic Institute, and then at Goskino, the State Cinema ministry. He returned to those same halls where he had once met with Shumiatsky, Dukelsky, and Bolshakov, the commissars of cinema.

Times have changed. Goskino is falling apart, splitting at the seams. It may be disbanded soon. The movies are no longer the most important of the arts. Gorbachev and Yeltsin have no time to watch films (they may watch for entertainment once in a while, but they keep their opinions to themselves). There is no Master of the Movies anymore.

Many people, including Alexander Ganshin, have a hard time without a master. Life seemed simpler when one person's word was law. It was easier to let one man make all the decisions. It was much easier when all you had to do was follow orders.

TOP: *Line in front of the Hall of Columns, where Stalin's body lay in state.*
ABOVE: *Women crying during Stalin's funeral.*
RIGHT: *Memorial meeting for Stalin at Moscow University, March 1953.*
OPPOSITE: *Crowd filling Gorky Street during Stalin's funeral.*

Confusion had overtaken the Kolyma V.I.P.'s even before the announcement of the fatal outcome of the illness of our Leader and Friend. The preliminary news bulletins had already plunged the authorities into a state of agonized incomprehension. For they had completely overlooked the strange fact that the Generalissimo was made of the same imperfect flesh and blood as we sinful mortals. The very fact of his illness was a crack in the structure of that happy, intelligible, harmonious planet of which they were the denizens and the masters and which they so skillfully controlled. Blood pressure...albuminates in the urine...Damn it, that sort of stuff was all very well for ordinary mortals, but what could such base matters possibly have to do with *him*?

—*Eugenia Ginzburg:*
Within the Whirlwind

TOP: *Svetlana Alliluyeva.*

BOTTOM, LEFT: *Artists in the Hall of Columns record-ing the funeral.*

BOTTOM, RIGHT: *Vasily Stalin, at his father's funeral.*

OPPOSITE, TOP: *Left to right: Molotov, Voroshilov, Beria, Malenkov, Bulganin, Khrushchev, Kaga-novich, and Mikoyan with Stalin's body.*

OPPOSITE, BOTTOM: *Funeral cortege from the House of Unions to the Lenin mausoleum.*

OPPOSITE: *Military honor band on Red Square opposite the Lenin mausoleum.*

ABOVE: *Stalin's body being carried into the mausoleum. "Stalin" has already been engraved on the granite, underneath "Lenin." Stalin's body was removed from the mausoleum in 1961.*

I must admit to being an incorrigible optimist. Like those who believed at the beginning of this century that life had to be better than in the nineteenth century, I am now convinced that we will soon witness a complete resurgence of humane values. I mean this not only in respect to social justice, but also in cultural life and in everything else. Far from being shaken in my optimism by the bitter experience of the first half of this incredible century, I am encouraged to believe that all we have been through will have served to turn people against the idea, so tempting at first sight, that the end justifies the means and "everything is permitted." Mandelstam taught me to believe that history is a practical testing-ground for the ways of good and evil. We have tested the ways of evil. Will any of us want to revert to them? Isn't it true that the voices among us speaking of conscience and good are growing stronger? I feel that we are at the threshold of new days, and I think I detect signs of a new attitude.

—*Nadezhda Mandelstam:*
Hope Against Hope

TOP: *Andrei Konchalovsky, the director, with Aleksandr Zbruieve, who played Stalin.*
BOTTOM: *Claudio Bonivento, the producer, with Bob Hoskins, who played Beria.*

Andrei Konchalovsky: On the Making of The Inner Circle

I remember quite clearly riding my tricycle down the hall of the small apartment we lived in in 1943. It was six o'clock in the evening and Papa was in the bathroom washing up. The telephone rang, and Mama answered it. She said, "Yes, it is. Call back later, he's taking a bath. Who is it?" Then she put the receiver down slowly and went over to the bathroom. She banged on the door—Papa was in the shower and the water made a lot of noise. "You're wanted on the phone," she shouted. "Tell them to call back later," he answered. "It's Stalin," she said. The shower stopped. I remember this. The door opened and my father came out naked, covered with soap bubbles. He walked over to the phone, leaving wet, foamy tracks on the floor. I'd never seen my father like that—naked, soapy, and talking on the phone. He said, "Yes. All right. Of course. Thank you very much." I was struck by the fact that he didn't stutter. My father is a stutterer. He always stutters. But that time he spoke without a hitch. He was in shock. He replaced the receiver and said to mother, "Stalin wants me to come to the Kremlin."

That's my first real memory of Stalin's name. Why did Stalin call my father to the Kremlin? Because he liked the words father had submitted to the competition for a new national anthem. That was the first time he went to see Stalin—he was thirty years old at the time. At the age of twenty-five or twenty-six Stalin had awarded him the "Order of Lenin," for his poetry. He was completely unknown, but Stalin liked to promote unknown young people like that. My father went to the Kremlin to see Stalin several times. Stalin usually called people to the Kremlin at night. During the day he was busy with other things, and at night he liked to entertain himself. He would phone members of the intelligentsia—poets and writers. That first time they brought father back at five o'clock in the morning—of course I don't remember this part, but I remember Mama talking about it. The doorbell rang, and he virtually fell into Mama's arms. Drunk as a log. The man who brought father back was one of Stalin's special messengers, Mikhail Petrovich Lebedin. He now works as the head of the Mosfilm Fire Department. It was such an incredible coincidence. He was a consultant on my film. I didn't shoot a single frame in the Kremlin without his approval.

The idea that eventually became *The Inner Circle* arose in the 1960s when I met an old film projectionist named Alexander Ganshin at Goskino, where I had to screen my films for the censor. Once, just in passing, he said, "You think these are bosses. I know what a real boss is like, I used to show films to Stalin." I almost fell on the floor. "You mean you showed films to Stalin himself?" I asked. "I worked in the Kremlin with Stalin as his projectionist." I started going to see him fairly often. I was interested in this period. But at the time I didn't even think about making a film on it, it just wasn't possible. I told Ganshin he should write his memoirs. "Who cares about all that now," he said. "No one would publish them anyway." In the 1960s it was unthinkable. Even in the late 1970s, the part of *Siberiada* that touched on Stalin's death was cut out by the censor. So the idea just hibernated.

I left the country in 1979. For ten years I basically lived abroad. Theoretically, I could have made the film in the West, of course, but it would have been ridiculous. I couldn't make a film about Russia outside of Russia. A certain level of authenticity is absolutely necessary, and you can't achieve it anywhere else. Around 1987 or 1988, after perestroika was well under way and Soviet cinematography began to be freed up, I thought that it might now be possible to make such a film. Then a lot of Soviet movies on Stalin started appearing—there must be eight or ten of them by now. And people said to me, "There's already been so much done on Stalin, why are you doing another film? It's not interesting anymore." But still, it seemed to me that no one had seriously dealt with the question of what Stalin was for the

This series of **The Inner Circle** *movie stills, contrasting with actual photos shown here and throughout the book, demonstrates Konchalovsky's meticulous, documentary approach and attention to detail.*

THIS PAGE: *Movie stills of Sanshin (played by Tom Hulce) inside the KGB building.*

OPPOSITE PAGE: *This 1930s kitchen scene from the movie (*TOP*) bears striking resemblance to this contemporary photo of a Russian apartment today (*BOTTOM, *photo by Yury Feklistov).*

FOLLOWING PAGE, LEFT SIDE: *Movie still of Sanshin hanging Stalin's portrait (*TOP*) is similar to archival photograph (*BELOW*).*

RIGHT SIDE: *Movie stills of Aleksandr Zbruieve as Stalin and Bob Hoskins as Beria (*LEFT*) compared to historical photos (*RIGHT*).*

OPPOSITE: *Orphanage scenes from movie, with Lolita Davidovich as Sanshin's wife. (For historical photos, see chapter on children, pages 69-83.)*

THIS PAGE: *Stalin's entourage in movie (ABOVE) and in historical photo (BELOW).*

FOLLOWING PAGE: *Movie replica of House of Commons in Moscow (TOP); historical photo, March 1953 (BELOW). Stalin's body lay in state in the Hall of Columns in this building.*

nation, and what the nation was for Stalin. At this time I met the Italian producer Claudio Bonivento, who wanted to work with me. We became friends and decided to make a film. From the beginning Claudio was extremely enthusiastic about my idea. That's when I invited Soviet screenwriter Anatoly Usov to collaborate with me on a script about Stalin.

Ganshin served in some ways as the prototype for Ivan, but we certainly didn't follow his life in any literal way. Ganshin told me lots of stories, many of them even quite sensationalistic—details about Stalin's life at the *dacha*, Stalin's relationship with his daughter. About Stalin's private life. When you study materials like this so intensely for six months, any number of temptations arise, of course. At first I wanted to include all of this. But then I decided to narrow my focus. The narrower your focus, the richer and more profound the result. Anecdotes and stories that could have had extraordinary impact from a cinematic point of view—like Stalin's chat with Sergei Eisenstein, for instance—began to fall by the wayside. When my ideas began to crystallize, I realized that Ivan's life was more important than Stalin's. It would make for a less sensationalistic film, but it would be far more authentic.

This film is made from the point of view of an "innocent believer," a regular Russian guy, a real *homo sovieticus*, a person who has been voluntarily brainwashed. He, too, is a victim, of course, but he has been seduced. This is the main idea of the film, that Stalin in effect seduced the nation. The nation went into the Terror voluntarily. There was a little resistance in the beginning, but the country was broken very quickly, and then an extraordinary enthusiasm took over. Despite the terror, the arrests, and the Gulag, Stalin was revered by the people, revered by the great majority of Russian people. I'm not talking about all the other nationalities, the other republics. It's the Russian people and the Russian psychology that interests me.

If I couldn't answer the question of how a Stalin was possible in Russia, I at least wanted to ask it. That's why I started getting rid of the details about Stalin himself, and began to concentrate on Ivan's life. Then the theme of the Gubelman child arose,

the Jewish family, Ivan's wife, Anastasia. Crudely put, it's a classic love triangle. Anastasia loves Ivan, and Ivan loves Stalin. Beria is an extension of Stalin, and the child Katya Gubelman is an extension of Anastasia. Katya embodies Anastasia's pain, her victimization. And then there's the Jewish question, which is still a major issue in Russia.

The character of the professor in the film is important to me, because he brings a philosophical dimension to the film: He knows that if there were no Ivans, millions of Ivans, there would be no Stalin. He's the only one who sees things clearly. The other two characters who understand, but less articulately, are Gubelman and Anastasia. Ivan is a symbol of the petrified spirituality of the Russian people, the hypnotized people who are willing to justify every horror. Anastasia's soul is alive, however; she has natural bursts of human emotion that come into conflict with the existing reality. In the end Ivan's soul also begins to thaw a bit. As we all know, when frostbitten parts of the body begin to thaw out, it's very painful.

To me, the most important story was the relationship of the slave, Ivan, to his tyrant, his idol. Why? Because emotional, spiritual violence is as devastating and as damaging as physical violence. The devil always uses his power to seduce, not to force. That's why one of the most crucial scenes in the film is the one with Beria and Anastasia. He doesn't rape her, though he could have. He seduces her. Spiritual tragedy occurs when you realize you've been seduced, because you are implicated in your own victimization. And in this sense, Stalin seduced the nation. People died with Stalin's name on their lips during the war. This seduction acquired a mass dimension, bordering on fanaticism, which is characteristic of Russians.

Film portrayals of Stalin, as a rule, have either presented an absolutely false Stalin, as in the Soviet films of the Stalin period, which deified him, or else they presented a "demystified" or caricature Stalin. But Stalin was a figure of truly enormous historical import. He defined the era. We will never say that Stalin was a political figure of the Pasternak era. We say that Pasternak was a

figure of the twentieth century. A giant of negative dimensions. I wanted to endow him with the real weight and significance of his role.

I looked at lots of photographs. It was important for me to look at his face, at his expression. I did a lot of research and watched hours of newsreels and film footage of Stalin. In one of the chronicles I saw a fascinating close-up of Stalin that revealed a lot to me, aside from the incredible details, showing that Stalin really had a dried-up hand, his left hand, and that one leg was shorter than the other. It was an amazing psychological portrait. Stalin was sitting at the presidium, thinking. It was shot from a distance. Suddenly there's a vague blur in the foreground. Someone was moving in Stalin's direction. Stalin doesn't notice at first. Then he sees that someone is approaching him, and you see a totally predatory look flash in his eyes, like a lynx or a tiger. He instantly assesses the situation. We still don't know who's approaching him. But all of a sudden his face softens and takes on a kind, fatherly demeanor. It was a woman, a peasant from Uzbekistan. His whole personality was contained in that transition. It could have been a terrorist approaching to kill him, or one of his underlings who had to report something, but it turns out to be one of the people, and he immediately transforms himself into a knowing, affectionate godfather with a warm light twinkling in his eyes.

In another film clip, Stalin was going to vote. There were two voting urns. A close-up camera stood opposite the urn with the best lighting. Stalin and Molotov were approaching to vote. Molotov goes to the one with the camera because Stalin went to the other one. The filmmakers obviously thought Stalin would go to the well-lit urn. Molotov approaches and then he sees that that's where the camera is. He looks at Stalin, who is

poet of the Stalinist period. I wanted to create a character that might even be a bit exaggerated, because he is seen through Ivan's eyes, but who would be a figure of appropriately mythical proportions. This mythological Stalin, a living god, was in fact a reality for millions of people. I wasn't interested in showing him taking off his socks, or brushing his teeth. Stalin was a major slightly out of focus. Molotov stops, he doesn't know what to do. He hesitates, he doesn't want to cast his ballot. You can tell he wants to say, "Iosif Vissarionovich, you should vote over here," but Stalin doesn't look at him. I could just imagine what the cameraman was going through. A heart attack. There's a second, wide-shot camera, but it doesn't show much. Stalin approaches the second urn, and Molotov sees that there's no way out. So he goes to the urn opposite the close-up camera. He's uneasy, he's probably thinking, "This is it, they'll get rid of me tomorrow." He casts his ballot, and from the wide-shot camera you can see Stalin looking at Molotov, realizing that something unpleasant has happened. Stalin looks around to see where the cameras are located, smiles into his mustache, votes, and leaves. There was an extraordinary diplomatic tension in this little scene—it was charged with life, death, fate, everything. These two film clips and the sense of danger they conveyed, had an enormous impact on me. You can't see the danger, but you feel it. It's in the air. This is important in movies where death is present but unseen. *The Godfather* has that presence. But *The Godfather* only involved a conflict between two gangs—whereas Stalin could command an entire country and its people.

I was also fascinated to see how charming Stalin could be. He had a very infectious laugh. When he started laughing, everyone laughed. He liked jokes. My father, for instance, was absolutely entranced by him. He told us how Stalin laughed; my father would tell jokes and funny stories and Stalin laughed. They always drank a lot of wine. Stalin liked his guests to be drunk, because it relaxed them, and he liked this.

I wanted people to understand why Ivan and the Russian people adored Stalin. It wasn't just because he was powerful, but because on a personal level Stalin knew how to talk to people. He could be very crude with Beria or Voroshilov, for instance, but he was very affectionate with simple people. And that's an interesting detail. He had very few friends, except for the members of the Politburo, who were considered his friends. But he was afraid of them, he got rid of them. On the other hand, he seems to have genuinely loved and respected his guards, from all accounts. They were all simple Ivans, mostly from the countryside. He liked them be from the countryside because they hadn't been corrupted by city politics. He knew he could rely on them. Also, he thought it was democratic to talk to these simple people.

Stalin isn't just a one-dimensional statue in the film. I tried to make him radiate power. Like a king. And there's always something fatherly about him. I gave the actor one set of instructions. Talk to Ivan as if you were coming on to a woman. There should be a spark in your eye as if you were coming on to a woman. Make him fall in love with you. Stalin was good at this.

The less we saw of Stalin in the film, the more important I felt it was for everything to be authentic. This documentary approach can be seen if you look at the photographs. You can compare the scenes in the film and in the photos. We built a set of the screening room, but the rest was filmed in the Kremlin itself. In the courtyards and the inner corridors. That's why I was so interested in the photographs. I wanted to know just exactly how Stalin walked around the Kremlin. This was the first time permission was given to shoot in these buildings—the Party apparat buildings, the part of the Kremlin where Stalin lived and worked. No one had shot there before. And then we were the first to get permission to film inside the KGB. That hall with the Lenin head is actually inside Lubianka, the KGB building. But the outside of the building is the Frunze Military Academy, because I wanted a Socialist Realist look. The esthetics of Stalinism were very close to those of German Fascism. That dry, imperial style is expressed in two images in the film, in Mukhina's sculpture of "The Worker and the Peasant," and in the "KGB" building. In terms of esthetics, the building of that sculpture, in the documentary footage at the beginning of the film, is very important for me. It symbolizes the government ideology, in which ideal people were supposed to be made of steel.

I tried to re-create the world inside the Kremlin with documentary scrupulousness. I was interested in details, like how the screenings were set up, what candies were on the table. Mikhail Petrovich, the man who brought my father home the night Stalin called him to the Kremlin, would come and say this is where the candies were, there was a chair here, a table there, officers didn't stand there. I didn't shoot anything without him. Everything was exactly reproduced. And this exactitude creates a certain naturalistic surrealism. The preparation of the screening room before Stalin's arrival takes ten minutes in the film. In *Rambo* you would have had ten scenes in that time. The accumulation of details conveys the intense, unreal atmosphere created by terror, which becomes a metaphor for what's happening in the country at large. That's why the bottle cap in that scene, for instance, is very important for me. The loose bottle cap. "You missed it, fucker," Vlasik says. That kind of detail reveals the hierarchy of terror, of fear. Another seemingly minor, but important, detail is when Katya notices that a food tin had been placed over a portrait of Stalin in the newspaper and that there's an oily stain on his face. Ivan is embarrassed and he removes the tin. And Katya says, "Don't be afraid, I won't tell anyone." That is very typical—this almost pagan worship of the image.

We filmed fifteen weeks in Moscow. It was very difficult, especially for the Western actors, who are used to working very fast. I'm spoiled by American standards of film production. But we knew it would be hard, we were prepared. And Russian actors are extremely flexible. They are some of the best actors in the world—they have a kind of agility that allows them to play anything in any language, regardless of whether they understand it. Most of them knew no English. We worked by intonation, phrase by phrase. Basically, we were working as if it were sign language. On the other hand, the complexities of the story posed no difficulties for them, because they live in that world—Stalin is part of their own history.

The English-speaking actors read a lot in preparation. They worked hard, but in different ways. You don't have to know that much to play Beria. You're playing a powerful figure with a negative charge, who has to be quite charming. It wasn't all that hard for Bob Hoskins. It was far more difficult for Tom Hulce and Lolita Davidovich to play Ivan and Anastasia. But Hulce's personality—psychophysically, that is—is very gentle. He had no trouble understanding the horror of degradation. He wasn't uncomfortable being humiliated. It was harder for Lolita to understand Anastasia, because Lolita is an American woman raised in a tradition of women's liberation and a certain degree of equality. It was fairly difficult for her to get inside the consciousness of a Russian woman, which is almost Islamic in some respects—outwardly complaisant, very sacrificial. Russian women control men from behind the scenes. There is a kind of sacrificial quality that Russian people have, which is emotional rather than rational. And that was hard for Lolita. "Why doesn't Anastasia ever blow up....Why doesn't she fight back?" When they tell her that she won't see the child Katya again, she explodes and weeps, because she knows she must obey.

Beria is a figure who is permitted to be evil. He exudes authority and threat, he's Stalin's punishing arm. The difficulty in this film, from a director's point of view, was to show villains as seemingly normal people, without any obvious horror. Yet the viewer had to be certain that they are villains. It's a lot easier to show blood and gore than to show how everyone's afraid of Beria. As Beria, Hoskins had to emanate direct threat and terror, but wrap it all in smiles, winks, and jokes. Stalin seduced the nation just the way Beria seduced Anastasia. The difference is that Anastasia realizes that she's been seduced.

I was a bit nervous about doing the film with English-speaking actors. But it was the only way to go, I'm convinced. If I had made a film about Stalinism for Russia, in Russian for Russians only, I wouldn't have had to explain so many things. This film is very straightforward, almost documentary in a sense; it's an attempt to create a powerful metaphor through direct means. This is very unusual for Russia, where an artist is not generally considered serious unless he employs a very convoluted symbolism, a kind of provincial surrealism. If the film had been done in Russian, I could have used a complex, cryptic language, but it would have been as difficult for non-Russians to understand as it is for Russians to understand

James Baldwin and the problems of American blacks.

But after ten years of life in America, I've become more aware of the problem of mutual misinterpretation. Americans fail to understand Russians to about the same degree that Russians fail to understand Americans. For instance, a lot of Russians and Americans now think that if they have democracy and free elections in Russia, the country will immediately become just like America. They don't understand that democracy is based, above all, on respect for individuality. Russians and Americans have two very different mentalities. Living in the United States, I came to understand that it's really very complicated to explain the psychological problems connected with Communism, with the cult of personality, etc. Americans thought that the communist system was shaky, and that as soon as it fell, everything would be all right. But in many ways the system was a product of the people's mentality. And it's important for people to understand this.

That's why I decided to work with American and English actors, to make a film that would be seen in America and Europe. In countries like Italy, Spain, Germany, not to mention Eastern Europe—countries that have experienced dictatorship, that know what fear is—you don't have to explain as much, of course. It's not like England or America or Sweden, say, which only know these things through reading Orwell. But I wanted to make the film in a language that would be comprehensible. So I tried to formulate the story in an essentially emotional register, because emotions are universal—fear, love, loss, pain. I am moved to make films by the belief that it is possible to use unfamiliar subject matter to provoke familiar, intelligible emotions. I decided that the most understandable figure would be a man who adores Stalin. I wanted to explode Stalinism from inside, to show the sources of the cult of personality, the fertile soil on which the seeds of dictatorship blossomed. But this is a film for Russians too, of course, and it will be shown in the Soviet Union, though I imagine the impact will be very different there.

Frankly, I'm not much of an optimist regarding the role of art in the life of the people. I don't really know if this film will contribute to the process of de-Stalinization. I think that art offers an education in ethics more than politics. In that respect, this film should make Russians think about whether the sources of Stalinism are to be found inside themselves. That's the main question. The sooner the Russian people acknowledge their responsibility for Stalinism, the sooner they will free themselves from it. You have to understand your own illness. The German people have, to a large degree, acknowledged the sources of Hitlerism in themselves, they have experienced a sense of historical guilt. Even so, we now see neo-Nazi groups springing up in Germany once again. The Russian people need to experience the bitterness of the loss they have suffered, the loss of their culture, their religion, their class structure—the middle class was completely wiped out, for instance. But it's crucial that the people acknowledge this, the nation as a whole, not just the upper echelons of society. That's when the healing process can take place. Until this happens, the possibility of an authoritarian system reestablishing itself is quite real.

All the major characters in my films make mistakes, usually bad mistakes. I want the viewer to learn to love a hero who makes mistakes. This goes against the grain of much American moviemaking. Americans like white hats and black hats, good guys and bad guys—although this is a departure from the great classics of American literature, which are not at all simplistic in this way. The struggle of good and evil within a human being is one of my main concerns. And this film is about that struggle within an entire nation.

In the light of the recent events—the August coup—this film is a reminder that it isn't over yet. Certain external structures have been destroyed, which of course are very important to destroy. But the internal barricades, so to speak, the internal, spiritual supports of Stalinism in the nation as a whole, remain. Russia has made major progress in recent years, but it isn't over yet. We can't predict what will happen next.

—Based on an interview
by Jamey Gambrell, September 1991

Biographical Glossary

Alliluyeva, Nadezhda Sergeevna (1901-1932), second wife of Stalin; committed suicide.

*Alliluyeva, Svetlana Iosifovna (1925-), daughter of Stalin, writer; defected to the West in 1967. Her *Twenty Letters to a Friend* give unusual insights into Stalin's private life in the 1930s.

Beria, Lavrenty Pavlovich (1899-1953), Soviet Party and state official, head of secret police, 1938-1953, notorious for his depraved lifestyle; convicted of high treason and executed after Stalin's death.

Bukharin, Nikolai Ivanovich (1888-1938), Soviet Party and state official; falsely convicted of high treason and executed.

Chiaureli, Mikhail Edisherovich (1894-1974), Soviet film director, best known for epic films about WWII glorifying Stalin.

*Davies, Joseph Edward (1876-1958), U.S. lawyer and ambassador to the Soviet Union, 1936-1938; author of *Mission to Moscow.*

Dikii, Alexei Denisovich (1889-1955), Soviet film and stage actor, prominently featured in pompous epic Soviet productions of 1940s/early 1950s.

Dovzhenko, Alexander Petrovich (1894-1956), a leading Soviet film director.

Dzerzhinsky, Feliks Edmundovich (1877-1926), Soviet Party and state official, founder of Soviet secret police, partisan of mass terror.

*Ehrenburg, Ilya Grigoryevich (1891-1967), Soviet writer and public figure, instrumental in creating pro-Soviet atmosphere in Western intellectual circles in 1930s/1940s; best known for his memoirs (published 1961-1965).

Eisenstein, Sergei Mikhailovich (1898-1948), a leading Soviet film director; second part of his *Ivan the Terrible* (1945) was banned by Stalin and released only in 1958.

Ezhov, Nikolai Ivanovich (1894-1939?), Soviet Party and state official, head of secret police, 1936-1938, at the crest of terror; arrested and executed for "treason."

Frunze, Mikhail Vasilyevich (1885-1925), Soviet state official and military leader; died under surgery reputedly ordered by Stalin.

Fyodorova, Zoya Alekseevna (1909-1981), Soviet film actress, arrested after WWII for an affair with an American Navy officer.

Gelovani, Mikhail Georgievich (1892-1956), Soviet actor who made a career of playing Stalin in postwar films.

*Ginzburg, Eugenia Semenovna (1906-1977), Soviet writer, historian; arrested on false charges in 1937, released in 1955. Best known for her memoirs *Within the Whirlwind.*

Kaganovich, Lazar Moiseevich (1893-1991), Soviet Party and state official.

Kalinin, Mikhail Ivanovich (1875-1946), Soviet state official, a figurehead "President" of the Soviet Union.

Kamenev, Lev Borisovich (1883-1936), Soviet Party and state official; falsely convicted of high treason and executed.

Kapler, Alexei Yakovlevich (1904-1979), Soviet scriptwriter; was arrested after WWII for an affair with Stalin's daughter; released after Stalin's death.

Khrushchev, Nikita Sergeevich (1894-1971), Soviet Party and state official; head of the Party and the Soviet Union (1953-1964), started de-Stalinization; ousted by the Party conservatives.

Kirov (Kostrikov), Sergei Mironovich (1886-1934), Soviet Party leader and statesman. His assassination in 1934 (reputedly ordered by Stalin) became a pretext for mass terror.

Kosior, Stanislav Vikentyevich (1889-1939), Soviet Party and state official, arrested on false charges and executed.

*Kozintsev, Grigory Mikhailovich (1905-1973), Soviet film director, best known for his Shakespeare film versions.

Krupskaya, Nadezhda Konstantinovna (1869-1939), wife of Lenin, Soviet Party activist; tried to resist the deification of Lenin initiated by Stalin.

Lenin (Ulyanov), Vladimir Ilyich (1870-1924), leader of Russian Communist Party; in 1917 headed the October Revolution; laid the foundations of the Soviet state developed by Stalin.

Malenkov, Georgy Maksimilianovich (1902-?), Soviet Party and state official; in 1953 succeeded Stalin as President of the USSR; ousted by Khrushchev.

*Mandelstam, Nadezhda Yakovlevna (1899-1980), wife of Osip Mandelstam; two volumes of her memoirs give an extremely vivid picture of literary and public life in Russia during the years of terror.

Mandelstam, Osip Emilyevich (1891-1938), poet, arrested for a poem against Stalin; died in custody under unknown circumstances.

Mekhlis, Lev Zakharovich (1889-1953), Soviet Party and state official.

Meyerhold, Vsevolod Emilyevich (1874-1940), a leading Soviet stage director; arrested on false charges and executed.

Mikhoels (Vovsi), Solomon Mikhailovich (1890-1948), actor, stage director, a leader of Soviet Jewish culture; was killed by a truck in an accident staged by the secret police.

Mikoyan, Anastas Ivanovich (1895-1978), Soviet Party and state official under Stalin and after.

Molotov, Vyacheslav Mikhailovich (1890-1986), Soviet Party and state official; as Foreign Minister was instrumental in concluding the German-Soviet non-aggression pact in August 1939.

Mzhavanadze, Vasily Pavlovich (1902-?), Soviet Party and state official under Stalin and after.

Ordzhonikidze, Grigory Konstantinovich (1886-1937), Soviet Party and state official; presumably died of a heart attack.

Pasternak, Boris Leonidovich (1890-1960), poet, writer; Nobel Prize winner (1958). His novel *Doctor Zhivago*, published in the West in 1957, became the cornerstone of modern Russian uncensored literature.

Poskrebyshev, Alexander Nikolaevich (1891-?), Soviet Party official, Stalin's personal secretary (1931-1953).

Shcherbakov, Alexander Sergeevich (1901-1945), Soviet Party and state official.

Shelepin, Alexander Nikolaevich (1918-), Soviet Party and state official, head of secret police under Khrushchev.

Shumiatsky, Boris Zakharovich (1886-1938), Soviet Party and state official; in the 1930s, minister of film industry.

Shvernik, Nikolai Mikhailovich (1888-1970), Soviet Party and state official under Stalin and after.

Stalin (Dzhugashvili), Iosif Vissarionovich (1879-1953), head of the Party and the state, 1922-1953. Built the totalitarian Soviet system based on unlimited power of the Communist Party and secret police.

*Steinbeck, John (Ernst) (1902-1968), U.S. novelist, Nobel Prize winner (1962).

Trotsky (Bronstein), Lev Davydovich (1877-1940), Soviet Party and state leader, instrumental in founding the Soviet state; ousted and exiled by Stalin in 1929; assassinated in Mexico by a Soviet agent.

Tukhachevsky, Mikhail Nikolaevich (1893-1937), Soviet Marshal, arrested on false charges and executed.

Vlasik, Nikolai Sidorovich, Soviet general, head of the Kremlin Guard, instrumental in organizing Stalin's everyday life; arrested and exiled in 1952.

Voroshilov, Kliment Efremovich (1881-1969), Soviet Party, state, and military official under Stalin.

Yagoda, Genrikh Grigoryevich (1891-1936), Soviet Party and state official; head of secret police (1934-1936); arrested and executed for "treason."

Yakir, Iona Emanuilovich (1896-1937), Soviet general; arrested on false charges and executed.

Zhdanov, Andrei Aleksandrovich (1896-1948), Soviet Party and state official under Stalin; launched Party attack on arts and literature after WWII.

Zhukov, Georgy Konstantinovich (1896-1974), Marshal of the Soviet Union, Soviet military leader, instrumental in bringing victory on the Soviet front in WWII.

Zinovyev (Apfelbaum), Grigory Evseevich (1882-1936), Soviet Party and state official; falsely convicted of high treason and executed.

---

*Author of excerpts used within this book.

For Further Reading

Alliluyeva, Svetlana. *Twenty Letters to a Friend.* Translated by Priscilla Johnson McMillan. New York: Harper & Row, 1967.

Avtorkhanov, Abdulakhman. *The Reign of Stalin.* Translated by L. J. Smith. Westport, CT: Hyperion, 1974.

Conquest, Robert. *The Great Terror: A Reassessment.* New York: Oxford University Press, 1991.

———. *The Harvest of Sorrow: Soviet Collectivization and the Terror Famine.* New York: Oxford University Press, 1987.

———. *Stalin: Breaker of Nations.* New York: Viking Penguin, 1991.

Davies, Joseph E. *Mission to Moscow.* Garden City, New York: Garden City Publishing Co., Inc., 1943.

Ehrenburg, Ilya. *Memoirs: 1921-1941.* Translated by Tatania Shebunina. New York: Grosset & Dunlap, 1966.

Ginzburg, Eugenia. *Within the Whirlwind.* Translated by Ian Boland. Orlando, FL: Harcourt Brace Jovanovich, 1981.

Mandelstam, Nadezhda. *Hope Abandoned.* Translated by Max Hayward. New York: Atheneum, 1970.

———. *Hope Against Hope.* Translated by Max Hayward. New York: Atheneum, 1974.

Nekrich, Aleksandr, and Mikhail Heller. *Utopia in Power: The History of the Soviet Union from 1917 to the Present.* New York: Summit Books, 1988.

Solzhenitsyn, Aleksandr I. *The First Circle.* Translated by Thomas P. Whitney. New York: HarperCollins, 1990.

———. *The Gulag Archipelago.* Translated by Thomas P. Whitney. New York: Harper & Row, 1973.

Steinbeck, John. *A Russian Journal.* New York: Paragon House, 1989.

Tucker, Robert C. *Stalin as Revolutionary, Eighteen Seventy-Nine to Nineteen Twenty-Nine: A Study in History and Personality.* New York: Norton, 1974.

Index

Page numbers in *italics* refer to photographs.

About the Authors of The Inner Circle

★ Filmmaker ANDREI KONCHALOVSKY began working in the American film industry in 1985 directing such films as the Academy Award-nominated *Runaway Train, Maria's Lovers, Duet for One, Shy People, Homer and Eddie,* and *Tango and Cash.* Earlier in his career, Konchalovsky, whose father wrote the Soviet national anthem, studied at the Moscow Film School and later teamed up with Andrei Tarkovsky, one of the most internationally renowned of Soviet filmmakers, to produce several movies. His own work grew more artistically daring and innovative; one film was banned by Soviet censorship in 1966, only to be shown 11 years later at the Moscow Film Festival. His highly respected work is followed by knowledgeable filmgoers the world over.

★ Writer ALEXANDER LIPKOV was born in Moscow in 1936, and is the author of numerous screenplays, books, and articles, primarily on Soviet film. He has written on the work of Konchalovsky for 25 years; a collection of his writing with and about the filmmaker will be published soon in English.

★ Editor and translator JAMEY GAMBRELL is currently a contributing editor to *Art in America* magazine. The author of numerous articles on Russian literature and art, her work has appeared in *The New Yorker*, *The New York Review of Books*, and *Artforum*. She has also translated into English the work of Joseph Brodsky, Marina Tsvetaeva, Tatyana Tolstaya, plus many others.